T0007505

Much has been written ab[...] ment of immigrants from south of the Rio Grande once they have entered the United States. But this account, by the itinerant, effervescent and highly original journalist Belén Fernández, offers a quite different take.

In this concise, vivid account Fernández shows us what life is like for would-be migrants, not just from the Mexican side of the border, but inside Siglo XXI, the notorious migrant detention center in the south of the country.

Journalists are prohibited from entering Siglo XXI; Fernández only gained access because she herself was detained as a result of faulty travel documents. Once inside the facility, Fernández was able to speak with detained women from Honduras, Cuba, Haiti, Bangladesh, and beyond. Their stories, detailing the hardships that prompted them to leave their homes, and the dangers they have experienced on an often-tortuous journey north, form the core of this unique book. The companionship and support they offer to Fernández, whose antipathy to returning to the United States, the country they are desperate to enter, is a source of bemusement and perplexity, displays a generosity that is deeply moving.

In the end, the Siglo XXI center emerges as a strikingly precise metaphor for a twenty-first century in which poor people, effectively imprisoned by punitive US immigration policies, nevertheless display astonishing resilience and camaraderie.

PRAISE FOR BELÉN FERNÁNDEZ

"With wickedly dry humor, Fernández uses her time being held inside a notorious migrant detention center in Mexico—she fears being deported back *to* the U.S.— to examine America's own ventures abroad and lack of respect for borders. Her prose is concise, not a wasted word, worthy of Orwell. An intrepid wanderer and journalist, a P. J. O'Rourke of the left." —Raymond Bonner, former *New York Times* foreign correspondent and author of *Weakness and Deceit: American and El Salvador's Dirty War*

"I doubt there's another journalist quite like her . . . Fernández's prose is so incisive, pithy, powerful, and often funny." —*Counterpunch*

"A dangerously enchanting siren." —Francisco Goldman

"A searing indictment of the violence of the U.S. funded de facto border in southern Mexico, and the transformation of Tapachula, Mexico into a jail-city. This page-turner will leave you not knowing whether to laugh or to cry, but certain that Siglo XXI and all other cages must be burned to the ground." —Tanya Maria Golash-Boza, author of *Deported*

"A chilling vision of the 'imperial fucking holding pen' in México, where the U.S. exportation of public misery meets Fernández's penetrating critique. Precisely in a moment when we need more and better knowledge about how US policies perpetuate police death, mass incarceration and imperial femicide, Fernández's unsettling book gives it to us." —Jeffrey Herlihy-Mera, Professor, Universidad de Puerto Rico-Mayagüez

"Inside Siglo XXI is a personal, detailed, heart-wrenching, and often bitingly hilarious account of the innards of the U.S. empire. There is not a writer who can detail both the absolute absurdity and dehumanizing brutality of U.S. imperialism, often in the same exact sentence, as well as Belén Fernández. For anyone who wishes to understand how the U.S. immigration and border regime really works outside of its boundaries, this book vividly lays it out." —Todd Miller, author of *Empire of Borders*

INSIDE SIGLO XXI

INSIDE
SIGLO
XXI

Locked Up in Mexico's Largest Immigration Detention Center

BELÉN FERNÁNDEZ

OR Books

New York · London

© 2022 Belén Fernández

Published by OR Books, New York and London
Visit our website at www.orbooks.com

All rights information: rights@orbooks.com

All rights reserved. No part of this book may be reproduced or transmitted
in any form or by any means, electronic or mechanical, including photocopy,
recording, or any information storage retrieval system, without permission in
writing from the publisher, except brief passages for review purposes.

First printing 2022

Library of Congress Cataloging-in-Publication Data: A catalog record for this
book is available from the Library of Congress.
British Library Cataloging in Publication Data: A catalog record for this book
is available from the British Library.

Typeset by Lapiz Digital.

paperback ISBN 978-1-68219-355-6 • ebook ISBN 978-1-68219-356-3

For my lovely Mama, again

CONTENTS

1: CHECKED IN, CHECKED OUT

On July 11, 2021, I arrived by car to Tapachula International Airport in the Mexican state of Chiapas—a grandiose title for the diminutive compound and runway plunked down amidst tropical vegetation just west of Mexico's border with Guatemala—for what was meant to be my return flight to the neighboring state of Oaxaca, where I had taken up accidental residence at the start of the pandemic the previous year.

I had come to Tapachula for four days with a vague plan to write something about migrants, of which there were plenty. During my initial excursion to the city center, the woman who served me juice at a market stall reported that, out of every ten people nowadays, five were Haitian, three were Cuban or something else, and two were *chiapanecos*. Gesturing at the ground beyond the stall, she remarked: "Sometimes at night it seems like a hotel around here, with people sleeping all over." After attending to the *licuado* orders of the pair of Cuban men seated next to me in Brazil soccer tank tops and flip-flops, the woman proceeded to entertain me with stories of coronavirus dishwashing protocols and their effects on her now bleach-burned hands.

Plagued by an almost neurotic aversion to behaving like a journalist, I had spent the morning wandering awkwardly around and inventing pretexts to talk to people, like the young Haitian man on a bench who could not tell me how to get to the market but who patiently put up with me as I swung the conversation in other directions. He had arrived at Tapachula a month earlier from Brazil, a distance of several thousand kilometers, much of which he had traveled on foot. Obviously, he said, he would have preferred to be at home in Haiti; doesn't everyone want to be in their own home? He gazed at a point over my shoulder and shrugged with a resigned smile—a shrug that better encapsulated the arbitrary cruelty of a world defined by borders than anything I could ever write.

Another of my interlocutors was a young Nicaraguan with "Juan 3:16" tattooed on the side of his neck—a reference, Google later informed me, to the Bible verse according to which "God so loved the world that he gave his one and only Son, that whoever believes in him shall not perish but have eternal life." This young man had worked in radio in Nicaragua, and, putting on a deep voice, performed a rapid-fire dedication "to Belén in Tapachula" as he accompanied me in search of the Coppel department store that I urgently needed to find.

Our stroll was briefly interrupted when Juan 3:16 had to chase down the Mexican youth who had relieved a distraught schoolgirl of her mobile phone. Upon his return, he recounted to me the highlights of hitchhiking through Honduras and Guatemala to Mexico, where he was promptly apprehended on a minibus by Mexican immigration officers.

He would have liked to have made it somewhere cold, like Michigan, he said, but instead he ended up imprisoned for twenty-three days in Tapachula's notoriously overcrowded and abuse-ridden *estación migratoria*—"migration station"—which had thanks to the either witting or unwitting irony of a previous Mexican government been christened Siglo XXI, meaning "twenty-first century." Inside, he had apparently contracted COVID—or at least that is what he had deduced from his inability to breathe for various days—but reckoned that the psychological torment had been just as bad or worse. He had since applied for asylum in Mexico and was now sleeping indefinitely on the streets of Tapachula awaiting his next appointment with COMAR, the Mexican Commission for Refugee Assistance, while also endeavoring to recuperate his confiscated video camera from the dark void into which it had been disappeared by immigration personnel.

I had heard, of course, of Siglo XXI, a facility listed on the website of the Geneva-based Global Detention Project as having these "inadequate conditions": temperature; access to clean drinking water; showers and toilets; access to internet; access to telephones; bedding and clothing; cell space; food provision; hygiene; medical care; overcrowding; solitary confinement; and protection from physical injury. In the "outcomes" section of the listing, the boxes corresponding to "reports of deaths" and "reports of suicide attempts" are both marked "Yes."

As the Associated Press reported back in 2019, Siglo XXI—said to be Latin America's largest immigration detention center—is a "secretive place off-limits to public scrutiny where cellphones are confiscated and journalists aren't allowed inside." The AP had itself been denied access but had heard testimony according to which "women slept in hallways or in the dining hall among rats, cockroaches and pigeon droppings, as children wailed, mothers reused diapers and guards treated everyone with contempt."

When I brought up Siglo XXI to the friends I was staying with in Tapachula—we'll call them Diego and Polo, both employees of an immigrant rights organization—Polo offered to drive me past the facility, located on the northern outskirts of the city towards the Tacaná volcano. Assuming that this would be the closest I'd ever get to twenty-first-century barbarity, I peered through the car window at the looming complex—an appropriately symbolic landmark in a city Polo had dubbed "Atrapachula" based on its service, in his own unminced words, as an "imperial fucking holding pen" and trap for United States-bound migrants, with the U.S. bullying Mexico into performing its dirty work against people often fleeing U.S.-fueled catastrophe in the first place.

I jotted down some notes about Siglo XXI as a migrant prison within the migrant prison of Tapachula, and figured I had enough material for at least an article or two cataloging the latest migrant-related transgressions of my heinous homeland to the north. On the morning of my scheduled return to Oaxaca, I paid a guilty visit to that imperial outpost known as Walmart, where I acquired bread and a giant slab of industrial Manchego cheese for my trip as well as two bottles of wine, which I assumed Diego and Polo would assist in consuming prior to my departure. When they proved less than helpful on that front, occupied as they were with preventing the cat from devouring an injured bird in the backyard, most of the work fell to me—meaning that I was in spectacular shape by the time they dropped me off at the airport, and at first thought nothing of it when a female immigration officer requested my *forma migratoria múltiple*, or Mexican entry permit, something that had never before happened on a domestic flight.

I busied myself scrolling through Facebook on my phone while other passengers streamed past me to the security check and the immigration officer—we'll call her Migra 1—alternately inspected my passport, my *forma migratoria*, and her computer. Through my wine-altered state, I eventually perceived that an extraordinary amount of time had elapsed, and made eye contact with Migra 1, who with raised eyebrows advised me that neither my *forma* nor the June 2021 entry stamp in my passport were "in the system." In fact, she said, my last appearance in the system was March 2020—which was indeed the last time I had actually entered Mexico rather than lazily relying on some dude in Mexico City to provide me with a falsified *forma migratoria* and entry stamp after my initial visa had expired. In an effort to save my ass, I mustered my best self-righteous gringa demeanor, rolled my eyes in exaggerated fashion, and requested that the "system" sort itself out as quickly as possible as I had places to be. I then retired a few meters and frantically phoned the Mexico City dude, who did not answer, and Diego, who did—and who said something to the effect of: "Oh, shit."

The next thing I knew, I was being ordered to turn off my phone as Migra 1 and Migra 2, a man, escorted me to a small back room with a desk and Xerox machine. From that point on, my recollection of events is a blur, but I have been able to piece them together thanks to several pages of notes scribbled in real time. Granted, my decision to whip out a pen was perhaps a result not so much of foresight as of a need to project importance— and, in case Migras 1 and 2 had not adequately received the message, I announced that I was a journalist and would be writing about this whole episode. According to my notes, I also announced that I would just walk out of the airport and be done with it all, but was told that such behavior would occasion the summoning of the National Guard.

After reflecting for a couple of lines on the novelty of not having my way, I apparently switched gears and got a little bit excited about the inside view I had finagled of the migrant detention apparatus. Some notes ensued on the serendipity of my misfortune, interspersed with expressions of culpability re: the grotesque privilege obviously enjoyed by anyone who is able to experience excitement at being detained. I could not have asked for a better scoop on Atrapachula, I gushed to my notebook, than being *atrapada* myself (or would it be *atrapachulada*?). I tried interrogating my interrogators, but this produced little information aside from that Migra 1 had worked in immigration for four years and liked it, that cross-border migration from Guatemala had indeed been on the rise, and that some "illegal" migrants had attempted—like me—to fly out of Tapachula airport. When I asked if the migrant-trapping orders originated in the U.S., Migra 2 nodded but then revised his response to the noncommittal: "We do not have that information." Nor was he cooperative when I sought to establish whether the "*GOOOOOOOOLLLLL*" that emanated from a television set somewhere in the airport corresponded to Italy or England, and simply stared at the wall.

At some point, it occurred to me that I might be deported to the United States—with this precise moment recorded in my notebook as: "fuck are they going to deport me can you imagine haha." In addition to not having lived in the U.S. since graduating college in 2003, I hadn't set foot in the country in six years—not even transiting through its airports—as I found it to be irreparably creepy and hazardous to my mental health. The U.S. is itself mentally ill, and there is perhaps no better indication of this than that it is the only place in the world where students are regularly massacred at school—a phenomenon that has to do with more than just the ludicrous ease with which armaments can be procured. When I was growing up in Austin, Texas, I thought it was entirely normal for eight-year-old me to be shooting beer cans off fenceposts with my parents' friend's pistol. I also became well acquainted with the soulless consumerism that passes for culture in the U.S., and the idea that life is a competition as opposed to a communal collaboration—a brutal dog-eat-dog arrangement that fuels individual alienation and is clearly not helped by the government's penchant for spending trillions of dollars on wars abroad rather than on, say, physical and mental healthcare for the domestic population. But a sick society is ultimately more profitable for the arms and pharmaceutical industries that underpin U.S. capitalism, and business proceeds as usual.

Resuming my state of panic in the back room of the Tapachula airport, I had begun sketching notes about how to sneak back into Mexico by land from Texas when Migra 1 declared that my ride had come. Motioning for me to gather my bags, she escorted me out of the airport to a waiting van, saying only that I would be taken to a *centro migratorio* where my "situation" would be "resolved."

I climbed into the van, the back row of which was occupied by a young Honduran woman from San Pedro Sula, whose small son was sleeping in her lap. They had been traveling for five days straight, she told me, and had been detained on a bus outside Tapachula by immigration officials. The only hope now, she said, was to apply for asylum in Mexico, as the excessive crime rate in Honduras ruled out the possibility of return. Giggling politely at my suggestion that even the Honduran president—U.S. narco-buddy Juan Orlando Hernández—was a criminal, she shifted her son on her lap as I took a seat in the front row of the van and peered through the grated partition at Migra 3, the driver, and the member of the National Guard who was occupying the passenger's seat.

Glancing back over his shoulder, the Guardia Nacional asked where I was from—and then swung fully around to stare at me in shock after hearing the answer, which didn't do much to assuage my feelings of self-hatred at the superior value my passport automatically conferred upon my life. "What are you *doing* here?" he inquired amusedly, and went on to express his opinion that I would certainly be deported—but that, not to worry, it would be free of charge! First, however, my situation had to be resolved. I don't recall the exact moment at which I realized where I was being taken, but it must have been shortly after Migra 3 put the van in motion. At any rate, the epiphany is forever preserved in my notebook as: "FUCK. SIGLO XXI."

2: ON THE SOUTHERN BORDER

FROM THE SOUTHERN BLOCKS

Had I not been thrown in jail, I would have begun my report from Tapachula with a description of the golden statue of a seated Benito Juárez—Mexico's iconic nineteenth-century leader and the first Mexican president of indigenous origins—that serves as a centerpiece of downtown. Behind the statue is a curved wall, on which is inscribed a quote from Juárez in capital letters: "*Entre los individuos como entre las naciones el respeto al derecho ajeno es la paz,*" meaning "Among individuals as among nations, respect for the rights of others is peace." It is a thought-provoking backdrop, to say the least, for a scene that embodies a definitive lack of respect on both fronts—both in terms of the harsh conditions facing individual migrants and the patronizingly destructive comportment of a certain global superpower, whose conversion of Mexico into a backyard migrant detention center is hardly the stuff of neighborly "peace."

The statement about *respeto al derecho ajeno* had transpired in the context of Juárez's "manifesto to the nation," delivered on July 15, 1867, when he triumphantly entered Mexico City following the defeat of Maximiliano de Habsburgo, the Austrian archduke whom Napoleon III had installed as emperor of Mexico in 1864. This, naturally, was far from the end of imperial meddling in the country—albeit from a different direction. Even Porfirio Díaz, the long-term Mexican dictator who died in 1915, is said to have remarked: "Poor Mexico, so far from God, so close to the United States."

Now, more than a century after Díaz's death, contemporary perks of geographic proximity have included the United States' ability to inundate Mexico with junk food and attendant health problems while ransacking the Mexican economy with so-called "free trade." As journalist Garry Leech writes in his chapter of the edited volume *Asylum for Sale: Profit and Protest in the Migration Industry*, the North American Free Trade Agreement (NAFTA), which came into effect in 1994, theoretically permitted agricultural subsidies by the three signatory governments. In practice, however, only the U.S. and Canada were eligible for this freedom—"a discrepancy caused by the broad neoliberal framework of global capitalism," specifically conditions placed on previous IMF and U.S. loans to Mexico. United States agribusiness was therefore able to exploit an egregious bias, "constituting further structural violence that shattered the lives of millions of Mexican small farmers through

NAFTA-sanctioned dumping of heavily subsidized US food products onto the Mexican market." In 2017, NPR noted that some two million Mexican farmers had "lost their land in the NAFTA era," while corn—a "staple food and a religious symbol for the indigenous population"—was now primarily imported from the U.S. Midwest.

The mass shattering of lives fueled a northward exodus, with economic refugees finding themselves up against an increasingly militarized U.S. border; after all, what's the point of wreaking international havoc if you can't contain the fallout? Leech suggests that the new-and-improved USMCA—the United States-Mexico-Canada Agreement, alternately billed as NAFTA 2.0 and birthed by U.S. President Donald Trump—might "be more accurately called the United States Migrant Control Agreement," prohibiting as it does the free movement of labor across borders while facilitating the flow of corporate capital. And yet this is still a bit of a lackluster name for a deal brought to us by the man who, according to the *New York Times*, "often talked about fortifying a border wall with a water-filled trench, stocked with snakes or alligators, prompting aides to seek a cost estimate. He wanted the wall electrified, with spikes on top that could pierce human flesh."

Another presidential vision, the *Times* reported, was for U.S. soldiers to "shoot migrants in the legs to slow them down."

Curiously, leftish Mexican President Andrés Manuel López Obrador (AMLO)—who prior to coming to power in 2018 had promised a humane migrant policy—chose none other than "*El respeto al derecho ajeno es la paz*" for the title of the section of his 2021 book *A la mitad del camino* (*Halfway There*) in which he discusses his "surprising" relationship with Trump. It is surprising, no doubt, to see the word *respeto* deployed in reference to the source of the opinion that Mexicans collectively are drug dealers, criminals, and "rapists"—and to see the self-declaredly "post-neoliberal" AMLO utilize the occasion of his July 2020 trip to Washington for the signing of the USMCA to propose revising the phrase attributed to Porfirio Díaz: "Blessed Mexico, so close to God and not so far from the United States."

In his recollection of the encounter, AMLO manages to simultaneously kiss imperial ass and endow his bout of ass-kissing with an air of victory, congratulating the "gentleman" Trump for his alleged respect for Mexican "sovereignty." Such was the level of camaraderie in Washington, apparently, that AMLO has felt compelled to include an endearing anecdote from the meal following the signing, where he says Trump bellowed—to much laughter and applause—"Now that there's no press I can talk about the wall!" He has also chosen to end the chapter with a "heartfelt thanks" to Trump specifically for sending him medicine when he came down with COVID, after the amulets he claimed were protecting him from the virus had failed to do the trick.

AMLO repeatedly pats himself on the back in *A la mitad del camino* for refusing to discuss Trump's beloved wall, although joking about it is evidently A-OK. So, too, is enforcing punitive U.S.-dictated borders, as long as you pretend that's not actually what you're up to at all. Preceding the euphoric USMCA blow-by-blow is a flashback to another episode in which AMLO portrays himself as an upholder of national sovereignty while basically doing exactly what the gringos tell him to vis-à-vis migrants. Having established at the outset of the section on *respeto al derecho ajeno* that Mexico is a country distinguished by "humanitarian acts"—with a lengthy history of offering "protection and asylum to persecuted people of the world"—AMLO describes the Trumpian tantrum of 2019 that nearly saw tariffs imposed on Mexican imports to the United States as punishment for Mexico's failure to sufficiently stem primarily Central American migrant flows (how's that for free trade?).

In the end, AMLO saved the day by standing his ground and pledging to be a better migrant-flow stemmer, "without violating human rights or completely closing our [southern] border and without becoming what they call a [safe] third country"—which, he explains, amounts to serving as a "big camp" for migrants waiting to receive asylum in the U.S. Never mind that the United States' so-called Migrant Protection Protocols, implemented earlier that year, turned Mexico's northern border into precisely that—albeit not at all safe and instead often a reproduction of the very geographies of violence that folks were fleeing—or that cracking down on U.S.-bound migration is inherently a violation of the human right to seek asylum.

To comply with Trump's demand that migration be cut in three months—or else tariffs!—Mexico's southern border was "reinforced with elements of the Guardia Nacional," AMLO writes, while the nation sought to "keep migrants in the southeast" to avoid a situation in which they arrived to the north and "ran the risk of being exploited by human traffickers" or even "massacred by criminal organizations." This, again, is a handy

humanitarian fig leaf for a fundamentally criminal policy: the erection of a de facto border wall—otherwise
known as Atrapachula—to trap vulnerable humans in
southern Mexico and prevent them from pursuing the
right or route to personal safety. Thanks to AMLO's
charitable concern for migrant lives, he informs us,
the trans-Mexico migrant flow was indeed reduced
by 75 percent in three months, thereby quelling the
tariff-tantrum from the north and ushering in an era of
jubilant U.S.-Mexican harmony.

What must the ghost of Benito Juárez be thinking, then, as his golden statue gazes out at downtown
Tapachula—which for a lot of migrants constitutes a
mitad del camino that will remain forever at the *mitad*?
According to the English-language version of visitmex-
ico.com, a website run by Mexico's tourism ministry,
Tapachula is a "city that embraces visitors with the
warmth of its people and wonders in every corner," a
place where "walking through its Historical Center is a
delight since besides breathing fresh air and enjoying its
warm weather, in your journey through its small streets
you will fall in love with the dozens of large houses
and art-deco residences." The Weather Spark site is
slightly more realistic in its assessment of the metrop-
olis as "hot and oppressive year round." To be sure, the

visitors I encountered in Tapachula's historical center on July 8, 2021—from Haiti, Honduras, El Salvador, and beyond—were being embraced by little other than a scorching sun, from which there was minimal refuge, particularly in light of the fact that significant swathes of shaded public space had been cordoned off with security tape under the pretext of coronavirus social distancing measures. Some migrants lingered around the fountain in the main plaza; a group of Haitians had seated themselves in front of the oversized colorful letters spelling Tapachula—obligatory clichéd photo op of Mexican cities big and small.

Many of those migrants who, like my Nicaraguan friend Juan 3:16, had successfully entered into the bureaucratic black hole operated by COMAR, the Mexican Commission for Refugee Assistance, were clutching folders containing papers certifying their spot in said black hole. On its own website, the United Nations High Commissioner for Refugees (UNHCR) provided instructions on "How to Apply for Refugee Status in Mexico," which began with the encouraging lines: "If you are afraid of returning to your country, you can apply for protection as a refugee in Mexico. The process is free and confidential." As Juan 3:16 and countless others had already learned, however, it was not always possible to initiate this helpful process before being placed indefinitely in jail and forced to undergo psychological anguish and physical abuse. The Washington Office on Latin America (WOLA) notes that, since COMAR asylum agents are not present at Mexican ports of entry and since persons presenting asylum claims on the border are generally detained by Mexico's National Migration Institute (INM, also referred to as Inami), "many asylum seekers try to travel undetected to towns close to the border to present themselves at a COMAR office or shelter. On this journey they are often victims of crimes including kidnapping, sexual assault, and robbery."

Under the section "Application Decision" on the UNHCR site, meanwhile, applicants were furnished with the following specifics: "COMAR will study your case. They can take up to 55 business days (Monday through Friday, not including weekends and Mexican holidays) after the date indicated in your certificate to give you the result. This term is divided into 45 business days to make a decision, followed by 10 additional days to inform you of the result. In some cases, COMAR may extend the deadline another 45 business days." Of course, the point of going into such hypothetical minutiae was called into question by the subsequent addendum: "Due to the COVID-19 health emergency, as of

March 24, 2020 and until further notice, these terms are suspended." Suspension of terms notwithstanding, aspiring asylees were required to "remain in the state where you submitted the application"—and to pay weekly visits to the local COMAR or Inami office to prove it. In Chiapas, the Mexican state with the highest poverty rate and few opportunities for migrants, this was a conundrum indeed.

The unsustainable precarity of the whole arrangement—whereby Tapachula was effectively converted into a "*ciudad-cárcel*," or "jail city," as many migrants began referring to it—would soon prompt the formation of migrant caravans attempting to break free of geographical detention. These were not to be confused with the United States-bound Central American migrant caravans of previous years, the first of which had set out in October 2018 from San Pedro Sula, Honduras, nine years after the U.S.-facilitated right-wing coup d'état against President Manuel Zelaya had plunged a country already suffering from decades of U.S.-sponsored physical and economic violence into ever more apocalyptic brutality. When news of the caravan emerged, then-President Trump took characteristically to Twitter to broadcast a "National Emergy [*sic*]," warning that "criminals and unknown Middle Easterners are mi own

National Emergency, xed in" with the procession—the implication being that a violent attack on the homeland was nigh. After all, there is no better way to attack the United States than by walking there from Honduras.

In August 2021, when desperate migrants began walking out of Tapachula, the Mexican government apparently detected the opportunity for its very own National Emergy, and Mexico's forces of law and order set about violently repressing the caravans. On September 5, the Miami-headquartered Spanish-language network Telemundo reported on unarmed migrants being charged at by the Guardia Nacional and kicked by Inami officials, while minors who had fainted were "dragged" to official vehicles. Telemundo quoted a Haitian migrant named Pierre on how it was not possible to survive in Chiapas "because they treat us like animals"; he went on to explain that the goal of the migrants comprising these caravans was not to cross the U.S. border but simply to extricate themselves "from this place" in order to look for work and be able to afford food, neither of which activity was currently an option.

But, as of my visit two months earlier in July, the *ciudad-cárcel* was still functioning more or less according to plan—or at least with no blatant, internationally televised challenges to its jurisdiction or the ethical comportment of its jailers. Before I ended up in Siglo XXI, it had not occurred to me that my own movement through Mexican territory might ever be curtailed in any way—such being my shameful normalization of gringo privilege even as I opposed it in theory. Granted, a semi-curtailment had taken place on account of coronavirus, when I had become stuck-but-not-really in the Oaxacan coastal village of Zipolite, where I had arrived in March 2020—just as the pandemic was taking off—for what was meant to be a twelve-day stay. The twelve days turned into one month and then six months and then a year, as a COVID time warp took hold and upended any lingering confidence in time as a solid and dependable construct. Weeks simultaneously flew by and dragged on forever, and eventually I stopped counting.

Mexico's "*Quédate en casa*" (or "stay at home") coronavirus campaign was never enforced in Zipolite—beyond some initial attempts by police to repel people from the beach—but for three months checkpoints to restrict access and departures were installed on either side of the village, including one directly in front of the apartment I was renting. I was issued a paper ID that permitted me to travel once a week to the nearby larger town of Pochutla, which boasted a Super Chedraui grocery store; however, given that the Super Chedraui abided by a municipal COVID-19 alcohol ban while the smaller shops of Zipolite did not, it generally made more sense to just stay put.

Despite the feeling of claustrophobia conferred by having a checkpoint in one's front yard manned by, inter alia, police and heavily armed members of the Mexican marine force, I was of course not literally stuck. For example, I could have very easily repatriated myself to the U.S.—except that I had spent the past seventeen years avoiding the place at all cost, as I pursued an almost pathologically itinerant existence that took me through continents and countries that felt more like home than my own alienated homeland. In the year preceding the pandemic, I had gone from Sri Lanka to Lebanon and Spain to El Salvador, with a dozen other countries in between. Still, I harbored an inexplicably existential aversion to having an official "home" or even a base, as though committing to a single identity in a single location would definitively put an end to all dreams, possibilities, and perhaps life itself. After a full year in Zipolite, I continued to squirm uncomfortably whenever it was suggested that I did, for all intents and purposes, "live" there.

And yet as much as I refused to abandon attachment to the idea of living nowhere—of embodying perpetual motion—I somehow could not force myself to leave Zipolite, even after the checkpoints had been dismantled and I was free to come and go. It was as if I had internalized the borders of the village, and I fretted not only about this newfound inertia but also about what kind of massively disturbed person whines about feeling trapped on a glorious Pacific beach. In an effort to recuperate my old ways, I booked a ticket to Turkey for September 5, 2020, to coincide with the expiration of my 180-day Mexican visa. My departure was thwarted when I proved physically incapable of packing my suitcase, and I settled for DHLing my passport from Pochutla to an enterprising immigration operative named Sergio in Mexico City, who came recommended by other lazy white tourists and whose bank account was reachable by deposit at any OXXO convenience store. Once an additional 180 days had elapsed, I repeated the procedure—all the while blissfully unaware that, although Sergio's handiwork sufficed for exiting the country without issue via the Mexico City airport, it was a different matter altogether in Tapachula.

In the meantime, the illusion that I was confined to Zipolite was all the more, well, illusory, given that I did manage to travel by bus for seven hours to Oaxaca City on several occasions, while also flying more than once to the Mexican capital as well as to Culiacán in the state of Sinaloa, home of the eponymous cartel. There I paid a visit to the chapel of Jesús Malverde, the legendary mustachioed Robin Hood-type figure who is generally cast as the unofficial patron saint of the narcos—but who is available for appeals from a wider demographic range, too. The shrine is fantastically over-cluttered with all manner of Malverde memorabilia alongside photographs, dollar bills, and handwritten notes tacked onto every surface thanking the pseudo-saint for favors granted; in one case, gratitude had been scrawled across a school diploma.

Once I had finished stockpiling Malverde bracelets and keychains and taken the requisite selfie with the solemn Malverde bust, an elderly man invited me to occupy the seat next to him—opposite the bust—that had just been vacated by another elderly man. We contemplated the scene in silence, until I asked him what sorts of prayers were usually fielded by our hero. Well, he said, if you have a drug shipment and you want it to arrive safely to its destination, you can ask Malverde to intercede. Or if you yourself are making a journey and want to arrive safely, you can also request his protection.

The shrine is no doubt ideally situated for migration-related pleas, located as it is directly in front of the railroad tracks along which runs *La Bestia*—also known as the "the train of death"—a network of freight trains that commences in Chiapas and has long been utilized by migrants making their way north. Traveling atop *La Bestia*, folks are vulnerable not only to assault and kidnapping by gangs but also to the possibility of falling onto the tracks and being crushed or decapitated.

My other main stop in Culiacán was the "narco-cemetery," Jardines del Humaya, just outside the city, which features ostentatious, air-conditioned mauso-leums that plenty of people would die to live in. The most expensive tomb-villa is reportedly the one housing the remains of the brother of notorious Sinaloa cartel founder Joaquín "El Chapo" Guzmán, who is him-self currently housed in the so-called "Alcatraz of the Rockies" in Colorado—since the U.S. has zero qualms about remaining up to its ears in the international drug trade while dramatically imprisoning token interna-tional drug lords.

The cemetery's humbly chatty groundskeeper, who approached me to verify that I was "not a YouTuber," was eagerly roped into satisfying my curiosity on a range of themes, starting with the tomb emblazoned with the Batman logo (the deceased narco-offspring inside had apparently been a fan). People came to Jardines del

Humaya from all over to visit, he told me, even from the North Pole and Oregon. He had inadvertently ended up on YouTube once, and the cemetery owners had not been pleased. No, you did not have to be narco-related to be buried at the cemetery; for example, there were three non-narcos who were buried together in one small grave. And no, he hadn't crossed the U.S. border in twenty years or so, but he used to run drugs to Arizona. This information was volunteered without allowing so much as a potential for stigmatization—but rather as a candid acknowledgement of what happens when your friendly neighborhood superpower destroys millions of Mexican livelihoods with its mythical "free trade" while simultaneously supervising a ravenous domestic market for drugs whose criminalization renders their trafficking lucrative. Obviously, the ever-increasing criminalization of migration has also caused profits to soar for facilitators of "illegal" cross-border movement. Back in the day, my interlocutor said, it cost five hundred dollars to cross from Mexico to the United States with a coyote, the slang term for people smuggler; now, it was ten thousand.

Shortly after returning from Sinaloa to Zipolite, I booked a ticket to Tapachula, southern Mexican epicenter of the U.S.-dictated migrant criminalization and detention regime, just beyond which lay the border with Guatemala. As American journalist Todd Miller writes in his book *Empire of Borders: The Expansion of the U.S. Border Around the World*, "this was where, as [gringo] officials have said, the United States border really began"— although, as is clear from the book's subtitle, the border in question did not really begin or end anywhere. The sensation that I had semi-recuperated my former itinerancy came as a relief, even as my movements were as yet confined to a single country. Being a writer focusing on things political, it also made sense to go more places where there were politics, instead of just beach.

I had other reasons, too, for selecting the *ciudad-cárcel* as my next destination. There were Diego and Polo from the immigrant rights organization, who had offered to show me the lay of the land in Atrapachula and along the Suchiate River that delineated the Mexican-Guatemalan border—pardon, the expanded U.S. border. And there was the fourteen-year-old from Tapachula—we'll call her Alejandra—whom I had promised to visit at her home. I had met Alejandra the previous year in Zipolite, where she had accompanied her mother to work for a couple of months at the small restaurant in front of the house I was renting from the restaurant owners. Alejandra and her mom stayed in a tent in the yard between house and restaurant along with Alejandra's four-year-old nephew, "Kevin," who, wise beyond his years, regularly scolded me for the horrifically unkempt state of my patio, for crying over worthless men, and for drinking too much wine. The scolding sessions generally entailed a placement of hands on hips, a shaking of the head, and an "*Ay*, Belén."

One day, Alejandra asked to join me for my morning jog on the beach. We had not made it two hundred meters before she had revealed that it had traditionally been her older sister "Fernanda"—Kevin's mom—who had accompanied their mother to Zipolite from Tapachula on annual work expeditions during the high season on the Oaxacan coast. This was no longer possible, Alejandra stated matter-of-factly, as Fernanda had recently been strangled to death in a Tapachula motel room at the age of eighteen by a jealous *militar*—yet another victim of Mexico's raging femicide epidemic that, as of 2020, was killing an average of ten women per day.

For the remainder of Alejandra's stay in Zipolite, we continued to jog together—or, when feeling less energetic, we'd sit by the soccer field on the decrepit, rusted swings that left a painful design imprinted on your ass and thighs for an hour after you stood up. I rarely spoke, but Alejandra had much to say, and would tell me about the times that she and Fernanda had fought and pulled each other's hair; about how her mother's screams had pierced the barrio when the news from the motel was received; about how her father, also a *militar*, had categorically blamed her mother for the whole killing. Pulling up her sister's still-active Facebook account, Alejandra would show me pictures of a smiling Fernanda in pink dress and bun or with superimposed animal ears courtesy of the cell phone camera. Sometimes, of course, the conversation was much lighter—and Alejandra would excitedly describe her barrio's pre-pandemic parties with all-night dancing and beer. It was important to exclude the Mejía family from these parties, she said, as they were known for drunkenly busting out their machetes.

Another topic of conversation was the migrant caravans that had begun passing through Tapachula in October 2018, prompting Trump's great "National Emergy" and causing a stir in the barrio as local media hyped the specter of marauding hordes—ever a handy tactic for distracting the populace from actual existential issues. To be sure, the propagation of a local emergy— and the "Othering" of migrants—was also politically useful in terms of dividing and conquering, as people like Alejandra and her family often overlooked the fact that they ultimately had more in common with Central American migrants fleeing violence and economic oppression than with, say, the member of the Mexican armed forces who had murdered Fernanda. During my subsequent internment in Siglo XXI, I would meet a Honduran detainee named Kimberly, who was not much older than Alejandra and whose two sisters had been victims of Honduras' own femicide epidemic, which had reached ever more brutal proportions in the aftermath of the 2009 coup. In typical fashion, the U.S. had cast the illegitimate right-wing post-coup regime as the Most Democratic Thing Ever.

Two days prior to my July incarceration—and, incidentally, three days after Tapachula had been rocked by a triple femicide, including one nine-year-old victim— I visited Alejandra, her mother, and Kevin at their house in Colonia Raymundo Enríquez on the outskirts of city. Faded school photos of Fernanda and Alejandra adorned the walls amidst religious paraphernalia, and a covered patio provided at least some respite from the stifling heat inside. The bathroom was behind the house, and lacked running water. A nebulous band of *hondureños* had taken up residence in the neighborhood, I was told, and Alejandra was not allowed out by herself after dark.

Reclining in a chair on the patio, Alejandra's mother joined me in overzealous consumption of the Modelo Especial beer I had stockpiled at the OXXO convenience store down the street, and dispatched Alejandra and Kevin to procure tortillas. Once they were gone, she informed me that she had to persevere for the sake of the children, but that sometimes life just didn't seem possible anymore. Then she raised her beer can to mine and laughed a laugh that was itself somehow childlike and uncynical.

Later in the afternoon, I was given a tour of the barrio, Kevin critiquing me all the while for stumbling down dirt paths simultaneously clutching two beers and one cup of liquor made from the nance fruit, which his grandmother had decided was another essential prop for the outing. I eventually said goodbye to Alejandra and family, promising to return for one of the non-Mejía parties, and made my way back to the house of Diego and Polo, who had been engaged in rather more productive pursuits than the overconsumption of beer. They had been on the phone with a group of Haitian migrants in Tijuana—the northern Mexican border city and de facto U.S. migrant holding pen that serves as Tapachula's corresponding imperial bookend—advising them on how to go about attempting to navigate the

U.S. system of asylum at a time when the country was effectively working to dismantle the very concept.

The website of the American Immigration Council notes that, while U.S. law clearly stipulates that anyone who is "physically present in the United States or who 'arrives' at the border must be given an opportunity to seek asylum," U.S. Customs and Border Protection (CBP) agents have categorically "turned away thousands of people who come to ports of entry seeking protection, including through a practice known as 'metering.'" This particular practice, which began in 2016 and was initially utilized primarily against Haitians at Tijuana's San Ysidro border crossing, saw CBP officers "assert a lack of capacity to refuse to inspect and process asylum seekers, requiring them to wait for weeks or months in Mexico just for the opportunity to start the asylum process."

Add to this Title 42, a sociopathic Trump-era policy dutifully continued by his supposedly less sociopathic successor Joe Biden. Using coronavirus as a pretext, Title 42 enables the U.S. to summarily expel asylum seekers without allowing them to apply for asylum, ostensibly in the interest of public health—even as U.S. citizens have been free to cross from the United States into Mexico and back as they please, whether vaccinated or not. Haitians have also been disproportionately screwed under Biden's application of Title 42, and U.S. border personnel have seized the chance to reenact scenes reminiscent of the good old days of slavery. Writing in *The Guardian* in September 2021, columnist Moustafa Bayoumi documented one such scene captured in a photograph from the Texas-Mexico border: "A white-presenting man on horseback – uniformed, armed and sneering – is grabbing a shoeless Black man by the neck of his T-shirt. The Black man's face bears an unmistakable look of horror. He struggles to remain upright while clinging dearly to some bags of food in his hands. Between the men, a long rein from the horse's bridle arches menacingly in the air like a whip."

When Diego and Polo got off the phone with the group of Haitian migrants in Tijuana—with whom they were able to communicate thanks to another Haitian migrant in Tijuana, who was not part of the group but who had volunteered to simultaneously interpret between Haitian Creole and Spanish—they filled me in on the details. The group had recently been attacked in their camp by men wielding knives, machetes, and sticks, and were now living on the street. The ambience of racism, violence, and insecurity had left them ever more convinced that their only option for self-preservation was to make it across the border to the U.S.—although being chased by white men on horseback is naturally neither very nonracist nor nonviolent.

None of the Haitian detainees I would soon meet in Siglo XXI—not to mention those of other nationalities—was overly impressed with my deathly fear of being deported to the country that many of them were risking their lives to reach. Charitably, however, they mostly restricted their reactions to hysterical laughter.

I was admitted to the detention center at approximately 6.01 p.m. on July 11, which I know from the sent time of the only text message I was able to compose in between the confiscation of my phone at the airport and the handoff of said phone by Migra 3—the driver of the jail-van—to Migra 4, the robot creature who received me at Siglo XXI. In the van, Migra 3 had promised that I would be able to extract pertinent phone numbers from my device upon arrival to the facility, although this was easier said than done and required a showdown with Migra 4, complete with tears on my part and a desperate plea for her to try to act like a human for a second. Two policewomen hovered over my shoulder and observed as I switched the phone on and copied my mother's Texas number into my notebook—and then sped over to WhatsApp to send the following two-line alert to Diego: "Sigko 21. Gelp." When Migra 4 was notified of this unauthorized internet activity, I was verbally assailed as though I had just dismembered a small child and was once again relieved of the phone, along with the majority of the rest of my possessions.

The 2019 Associated Press report came to mind, in which Sigko 21 had been characterized as a "secretive place off-limits to public scrutiny where cellphones are confiscated and journalists aren't allowed inside."

Whoops.

3: "DO NOT COME"

The Siglo XXI "migration station" was inaugurated in 2006, the final year of the presidency of Vicente Fox, a former CEO of Coca-Cola Mexico and a rather fine emblem of corporate conquest in a world where brown liquid flows across borders far more easily than brown people do. This is not to say that Fox himself did not sympathize with Mexican immigrants to the U.S., having charmingly remarked in 2005 that "there is no doubt that Mexicans, filled with dignity, willingness and ability to work, are doing jobs that not even blacks want to do there in the United States."

In its writeup of the inauguration on March 28, the magazine *Proceso* quoted Fox on his government's "humanist policy" vis-à-vis undocumented migrants intercepted along Mexico's southern border—a policy that would now be on display at Siglo XXI, where guests would be treated to "all the comforts," including human rights. Describing Mexico as a "land of immigrants," Fox chattered on about how Mexican society had been enriched by "people from different parts of the world" and how it was for this reason that his administration was so obsessed with respecting the rights of "those who pass through our territory in search of work and a better future." Granted, neither of these searches was easily conducted from inside a migrant prison—nor did the psychological torture of being put in indefinite limbo bode well for individual futures. During my own stay among "all the comforts," I heard more than one detainee declare: "I'm going to leave this place traumatized." This was no small statement, coming as it did from women who had already been subjected to sufficiently traumatizing situations in their home countries and on their respective journeys to Mexico.

Two days after the unveiling of the twenty-first century's most humanist jail, Fox met with U.S. President George W. Bush at the Fiesta Americana Condesa hotel in Cancún. And it was, it seems, one hell of an American fiesta. According to the transcript of the presidential banter appearing on the White House website, Bush thanked Fox for his "work to enforce Mexico's southern border" and his grasp of the idea that "border security is not just one country's prerogative; it's the prerogative and duty of both countries." The leader of the free world's recent efforts to obliterate any semblance of border security in Afghanistan and Iraq while slaughtering the inhabitants therein went on to congratulate Fox on his "fine job of. . . increasing the net worth of your citizens," which was "important for the American econ-omy, as well," because the "more net worth there is in Mexico, the more likely it is a Mexican may be wanting to buy a U.S. product." As an afterthought, Bush added: "And vice versa, by the way."

For his part, Fox (whose words appear "as trans-lated" by an evidently inept interpreter) took care to "mention with great satisfaction how productive the relation with the United States has been on bilateral basis, how the NAFTA, the Free Trade Agreement of North America has been, in order to promote develop-ment here in Mexico." In reality, of course, NAFTA's devastating effects on the Mexican economy had played a significant role in fueling the "border security" com-plex in the first place, predicated on the criminalization of cross-border movement by the victims of free trade. Coincidentally, 2006—the year of Siglo XXI's debut and the Fiesta Americana meeting—was the very same year that the powers that be undertook to implement the Central America-Dominican Republic Free Trade Agreement (CAFTA-DR), which involved Costa Rica, El Salvador, Guatemala, Honduras, and Nicaragua as well as, obviously, the DR.

As the Washington, DC-based consumer advocacy organization Public Citizen explains, "negotiations for

a U.S.-proposed hemisphere-wide NAFTA expansion"
had collapsed in 2003. Having witnessed how the whole
Mexico thing panned out, many in the hemisphere were
reluctant to get on board—to the great displeasure of
the "big pharmaceutical, agribusiness, oil and retail corporations that were reaping windfall profits under the
NAFTA model." The next best solution for the Bush
administration, then, was to "seek NAFTA-style deals
with a subset of Latin American countries they dubbed
the 'coalition of the willing.'" The war terminology
was certainly fitting, as CAFTA proceeded, predictably,
to replicate the destruction unleashed by its predeces-
sor, annihilating the livelihoods of rural farmworkers
and keeping urban wages nice and low. Anyway, who
said sweatshops aren't a great way of increasing citizens'
"net worth"? And surely having U.S. products literally
shoved down your throat is the same thing as "wanting
to buy" them.

It is perhaps less than shocking that Mexico's
National Migration Institute, Inami, was itself created
in 1993, the year before NAFTA came into effect. Then
Mexican president Carlos Salinas de Gortari, a Harvard
graduate and co-architect of the free trade agreement, was known for facilitating neoliberal pillage in
other ways, as well. In addition to overseeing a manic

privatization program, Salinas had dismantled Article 27 of the Mexican constitution, thereby effectively offering up communal lands for corporate plunder and reversing one of the key achievements of the Mexican Revolution. In her book *Border and Rule: Global Migration, Capitalism, and the Rise of Racist Nationalism*, scholar and activist Harsha Walia writes that NAFTA—accompanied as it was by frenzied border militarization—constituted an "extension of the Monroe Doctrine accelerating capitalist capture and colonial control." While free trade agreements are viewed as a "new phenomenon," she says, they in fact "perpetuate the pattern pioneered by the British East India Company of using trade to establish and subordinate markets for the benefit of imperial ruling class interests."

Doing his bit to advance imperial-ruling-class interests in Cancún, Fox followed up his ode to NAFTA and the myth of "development" with a recap of his administration's border security feats: "We are going after the criminals that are trafficking with people that are, let's say, promoting illegally the movement of citizens to the United States – the alien smugglers. We have stopped more than 120 of these criminals, alien smugglers." And yet the criminality did not stop with the alien smugglers: "Likewise, in the southern border, as President

Bush said, we are very active, very active on what has to do with patrol, constructions of different stations so as to stop migrants, illegal migrants, people that are coming illegally to the Mexican territory, and sending them back to their own countries with due respect to human rights."

Over the ensuing years, Mexico would get even more very active on the migration front. On July 7, 2014—exactly seven years to the day before I touched down in Tapachula—Enrique Peña Nieto, the latest right-wing zealot to become president of Mexico, enacted his *Programa Frontera Sur* ("Southern Border Program") with intense encouragement from the United States. Chiapas became saturated with militarized checkpoints, and human rights violations and deportations proliferated accordingly. The Mexican government website insists that the point of the *programa* was to "protect the lives of migrating persons and strengthen regional development."

In a 2015 assessment of Programa Frontera Sur, the Washington Office on Latin America noted that, while Inami agents were not equipped with lethal weaponry, this was not the case for "the Federal Police and other agencies that often accompany them." Nor were the INM folks totally emptyhanded, as they had reportedly taken to "using Taser-type electrical stun devices, and many of these 'non-lethal' operations have been quite brutal." American officials were downright "delighted," though—as WOLA put it—because, "whereas Mexico apprehended 67 percent more unaccompanied children from El Salvador, Guatemala, and Honduras from October 2014 to September 2015 compared to the same period in the previous year, U.S. authorities apprehended 45 percent fewer over this period." Such awesomeness occasioned the following tribute from Barack Obama during a 2015 rendezvous with Peña Nieto: "I very much appreciate Mexico's efforts in addressing the unaccompanied children who we saw spiking during the summer." Francisco Palmieri, Obama's deputy assistant secretary for Central America and the Caribbean, chimed in during a reunion of the U.S. Senate Homeland Security and Governmental Affairs Committee that same year: "Mexico has really been a key element in helping us lower the levels of unaccompanied children reaching our border since last summer. . . Mexico has really stepped up its game." And what a game it was.

In *Empire of Borders*, meanwhile, Todd Miller quotes a June 2018 statement by former CBP commissioner David Aguilar, in which he employed the U.S. establishment's ever-sophisticated denomination for non–Mexican migrants: "The last three years, Mexico has removed more Other Than Mexicans than we have." (For added sophistication, "Other Than Mexicans" is frequently shortened to "OTMs.") This deportation milestone was, Miller explains, bankrolled by the $3 billion U.S. military aid package known as the Mérida Initiative, the "third pillar" of which was "the creation of a 'twenty-first century U.S.-Mexican border.'" But what good is a twenty-first-century border without a twenty-first-century prison to go with it?

The website of the United States embassy and consulates in Mexico describes the purpose of Mérida's Pillar Three as "facilitat[ing] legitimate commerce and movement of people while curtailing the illicit flow of drugs, people, arms, and cash." To be sure, legitimacy of movement is far more freely conferred upon the citizens of an empire whose own infinitely expanding border is unilaterally marked as sacrosanct while the borders belonging to "Other Than Mexicans" and other Others are there for the penetrating. Miller observes: "Mexico had essentially become the U.S. Border Patrol's newest hire."

Fast-forward to 2021, and even more was "being done to accommodate the Americans," to borrow the words of a Mexican official quoted in an August Reuters article on a novel "air bridge" policy, whereby the Mexican government was flying OTMs from the country's northern border to its southern one and then expelling them into a remote area of the Guatemalan jungle. Some thirteen thousand migrants had thus far gotten to experience the air bridge, which had been inaugurated without so much as informing the Guatemalan government. The policy was being carried out "quietly," Reuters noted—a quietness that was no doubt helped by the fact that the media barely reported it despite its unmitigated battiness. Most of these OTMs were not Guatemalan, and were often forced to walk across the border in the middle of the night into a country to which they had no connection, much less local currency or a place to stay. Children and babies were not exempt from the arrangement. In some cases, migrants were expelled despite having already filed asylum claims in Mexico and being theoretically protected from deportation. Human Rights Watch documented an allegation from one expulsion victim who "said that Mexican immigration agents told her group they were intentionally being taken 'to the most remote border crossing' so they would 'learn their lesson.'"

Guatemala, of course, was also the site of U.S. Vice President Kamala Harris' June 2021 pompous lesson to persons potentially considering fleeing the country for their lives or otherwise migrating north to the U.S.: "Do not come. Do not come. The United States will continue to enforce our laws and secure our border." Violating the Guatemalan border, on the other hand, had long been just fine. In 1954, sixty-seven years before Guatemala was appointed a migrant dumping ground, the CIA orchestrated a coup against President Jacobo Árbenz, who was annoyingly attentive to the needs of the Guatemalan peasantry and insufficiently obsequious to U.S. corporate interests. The coup set the stage for a thirty-six-year civil war in which more than two hundred thousand Guatemalans were killed or disappeared, with U.S.-supported government forces committing the overwhelming majority of wartime crimes, including a scorched-earth campaign that eradicated hundreds of indigenous villages. While the civil war officially came to end in 1996, the earth does not unscorch itself overnight—and, as in Honduras, El Salvador, and elsewhere, the United States' destructive legacy in Guatemala continues to this day to influence migration patterns. In addition to being a non-solution, then, "Do not come" is profoundly morally fucked.

Harris' Guatemala jaunt came on the heels of fruitful collaborative regional exercises in "border security," i.e., some more bossing around by the United States of the governments of Mexico, Guatemala, and Honduras under the guise of "bilateral discussions"—the term used by White House press secretary Jen Psaki in an April 2021 press briefing. The discussions, said Psaki, had produced a "commitment," which in Mexico's case comprised the "decision to maintain 10,000 troops at its southern border, resulting in twice as many daily migrant interdictions." Guatemala, for its part, "surged 1,500 police and military personnel to its southern border with Honduras and agreed to set up 12 checkpoints along the migratory route," while Honduras "surged 7,000 police and military to disperse a large contingent of migrants." The military jargon was no accident—this was a war on migrants, after all—and Psaki went on to speculate: "I think the objective is to make it more difficult to make the journey and make crossing the borders more — more difficult."

It bears emphasizing that this particular strategy has never actually deterred desperate people from moving in the direction of perceived physical and economic safety, although it has certainly rendered their journeys more perilous. Just as Europe's fanatical border fortification policies have converted the Mediterranean Sea into an ever more populated migrant graveyard, U.S.

migrant deterrence efforts have had similar fallout in the Sonoran Desert, where undocumented migrants have been forced to navigate ever more remote and harsh terrain as safer routes are cut off. A young Mexican former migrant from the city of Oaxaca once described to me the disconcerting effect of coming across human bones in the desert—and yet the bones had not stopped him. Consider, too, the words of Norlan Yadier García Castro, a Honduran migrant quoted in *USA Today*: "Thousands have died in the desert. And if death doesn't stop us, will a wall? I don't think so." Sure enough, in April 2022—one year after Psaki's speech about making border crossings "more difficult"—the White House affirmed that there were "unprecedented flows of migrants from throughout the hemisphere" reaching Mexico and the United States. The previous month, U.S. authorities had arrested 210,000 migrants along its southern border, the "highest monthly total in two decades" as per Reuters.

Rewind again to March 2021 and another press briefing starring Psaki, during which she was interrogated about a spontaneous U.S. plan to "loan" Mexico millions of AstraZeneca vaccines in the midst of a significant uptick in migrants reaching the U.S. border. An excerpt from the transcript of the briefing on the White House website:

Q: So if I'm hearing you, the vaccine was given. Were there expectations set with the Mexicans that they help deal with this situation on the border?

MS. PSAKI: The — we —

Q: Was there a quid pro quo?

MS. PSAKI: There have been ex- — there have been expectations set outside of — unrelated — to any vaccine doses or request for them that they would be partners in dealing with the crisis on the border. And there have been requests, unrelated, that they — for doses of these vaccines. Every relationship has multiple layers of conversations that are happening at the same time.

By great coincidence, these multilayered conversations generally seemed to end with Mexico doing more or less what the United States wanted—which made it all the more interesting when the response from the U.S. embassy representative in Mexico City to my mother's request for assistance in springing me from Siglo XXI was: "We cannot tell Mexico what to do." After some sixteen or so hours in jail, I had finally been permitted my obligatory telephone call, and, feeling like a horrible child, had phoned my mom in the States. Unlike my father and me, who are prone to bouts of hysteria based on impromptu auto-diagnoses of invented illnesses (in 1971, for example, my dad had come down with knee cancer after eating canned beans, a brief medical hallucination from which he swiftly recovered without ever explaining the diagnostic thought sequence), my mother is good at controlling herself even in unimagined emergencies, and with forced calmness asked me how she should proceed.

As much as I did not want to involve the U.S. government in my predicament or be indebted to them in any way, I suggested calling the American embassy, as I had begun to fear that direct imperial intervention might in fact be my only ticket out. Other women had already spent a month or more in the facility, and the Inami official who was overseeing my phone call had warned me that I shouldn't expect to be released anytime soon—even for deportation—as the "*papeleo*," or paperwork, would take a good while. Obviously, my country would have to be notified, but it was anyone's guess as to when that would take place. I concluded that it could not hurt to have my mother expedite the notification process.

Mercifully in retrospect, my efforts to abuse my gringa privilege were thwarted when the Mexico City embassy refused to lift a finger on my behalf, as my mom would later document in a WhatsApp message to me:

"Btw the idiot at the embassy told us it would be at least 2 weeks before you got out of that place. He refused to take down your name, nor your passport number, nor your birthdate," because the U.S. "couldn't interfere." My father's WhatsApp messages were more dramatic, and involved an inexplicable capitalization scheme that was apparently the fault of a new and unfamiliar cell phone: "I Told That ASSHOLE At Embassy That You Had A Friend Who Worked At LA Jornada And Was A Big Shot Who TRAVELLED With The President" (*La Jornada* being a prominent Mexican newspaper and my Friend being the Mexican journalist Arturo Cano). Then there was the update: "Today We Had More Discussions With The ASSHOLEs at the embassy," which had entailed a female embassy employee hanging up on my mother after asking whether I was a *bona fide* U.S. citizen or just some naturalized María Belén Fernández.

According to my mother's WhatsApp missive, she had responded to the embassy's claim that "We cannot tell Mexico what to do" as follows: "I said really, since when." And indeed, Mexico's twenty-first-century migration policy—including the matter of the eponymous prison—has pretty much everything to do with the United States telling Mexico what to do.

4: LOCKED UP AND LACELESS

In the van from the Tapachula airport to Siglo XXI, in which the young Honduran woman from San Pedro Sula, her child, and I were the only detainees, the member of the Mexican Guardia Nacional in the passenger's seat had been most agreeable and responded to most of my comments with a "*Tienes toda la razón*"—"you're so right." First, I was right about how all American presidents were shit, some just more transparently so, and how there was money but no life in the U.S. Then I was right about how members of the Mexican Guardia Nacional should not be made to work forty-eight-hour shifts—which he was currently doing—as it made you crazy. Finally, I was right about how, if I had just taken the damn bus back to Oaxaca instead of flying, none of this would have been happening. When I asked how I was supposed to complete my work assignments from inside a jail, he cackled and reckoned, presciently as it turned out, that at least I would have plenty to write about later on—while Migra 3, the driver, informed me that it was not a jail at all but rather a "place to stay."

The Guardia, who hailed from Oaxaca himself, advised me to "relax" and try not to think too much because "we are here to protect you." The guards inside Siglo XXI would also protect me, he assured me, and would take my valuables for safekeeping so that they would not be stolen by "foreigners"—never mind that Inami officials had quite the reputation for appropriating foreign valuables. Notwithstanding the comment about foreigners, the Guardia asserted that all humans were equal and with equal rights, but that migration must be "legal"—which further turned the whole equality argument on its head given that most inhabitants of the world are denied the right to move "legally" and with ease through that world.

"What do you think?" he asked, turning once again to face me through the van's grated partition. "Are we all equal?"

"Of course," I said—not an enormously convincing assessment coming from the gringa who had just stupefied the Guardia Nacional by having been detained for an immigration infraction, while the detention of the Honduran woman and her son had been perfectly normalized in his eyes. I was so consumed with nervous chatter that I did not even register the moment that we pulled through the gates of Siglo XXI, the twenty-first-century monstrosity I had driven by with Polo just days before. The Hondurans were dropped off first at a section of the prison that the Guardia told me was reserved for mothers with children. Then it was my turn, and we pulled around to another entrance, where the Guardia bid me an encouraging adieu, as though he was depositing me at school on exam day. Migra 3 amiably herded me through the gaping door, where I was handed off to the two policewomen and Migra 4—who at least appeared determined not to give me any preferential treatment, and who from behind her desk set about barking orders as I felt any last pretense of free will drain from my being. Once my phone had been seized, we moved on to other matters.

Remove the laces from your shoes, she commanded, as I stared at her incredulously but did as I was told. The next command triggered a more neurotic reaction, and I begged Migra 4 to comprehend that, not only would the removal of my forty-plus bracelets be psychologically calamitous, it might also be physically impossible. For example, there was the formidable plastic red-and-gold glittery bracelet from a street vendor in the small southern Vietnamese beach town of Long Hai, which I had somehow wrested onto my right arm in 2014 only to never get it off again. This particular accoutrement had come to preoccupy my thoughts during the not-so-lockdown in Zipolite—where, without much else to do aside from get killed by the savage sea (Zipolite is even said to mean "beach of death" in the Zapotec language), I spent many hours lying in my hammock contemplating what would happen if I were to fall and break my right wrist. I imagined my hand and arm swelling around the bracelet as circulation was cut off, and wondered if I would be able to reach a hospital in time—or if any of the villagers might come to my rescue with a special plastic-slicing saw. If not, amputation of my arm might be necessary. I expressed my concerns to a neighbor, who suggested I could preemptively saw the bracelet off, but I was fond of the glitter and preferred instead to fret continuously about this and other eventualities such as having the ceiling fan fall on me while I was sleeping.

Now, seven years after the Long Hai bracelet had seemingly permanently welded itself to my person, I learned from the guardians of the twenty-first century that it could in fact be removed by slathering my lip balm from Barcelona over my hand as lubricant and then crushing a few bones. The two policewomen oversaw the bracelet removal operation, patiently undoing clasps and untying knot after knot—in other words, systematically dismantling me—as I whimpered helplessly to Migra 4 that these ornaments were *simbólicas* and she snapped back that, *simbólicas* or not, this was for my own *seguridad*. Off came the silver bracelet from Beirut that had become encrusted with Zipolite sand, the straw bracelet from Kampala woven in the colors of the Ugandan flag, and the purple bracelet from the Tbilisi flea market where I had also acquired assorted Lenin and Stalin paraphernalia and reflective sunglasses that gave me an extraterrestrial air. Off came the Jesús Malverde bracelet from the shrine in Sinaloa and the amber bracelet from downtown Tapachula. Then there were the myriad evil eye bracelets I had accumulated in Turkey, Albania, El Salvador, and Mexico and which I hoped sufficed in terms of self-protection in the absence of health insurance and martial arts training.

Once the bracelets had all been prised off, leaving swathes of garish white skin, it was time to hand over the valuables: money, computer, and battered iPod that briefly piqued the interest of Migra 4, who inquired after its gigabyte capacity. The valuables were cataloged and set aside for separate storage, whereupon the policewomen got to work emptying my duffel bag and backpack of all their contents, which were strewn across a concrete bench, dirty underwear and all. There was some temporary commotion over my gourd and metal straw for yerba mate, a substance to which I had been

addicted since the mid-aughts, and I was also interrogated about my deodorant as well as the jasmine oil
I used to compensate for said deodorant's lack of effectiveness. Little did I know that I would soon be provided with a miniature deodorant with the Inami logo
on it, which almost made the whole carceral experience
worth it.

Then my pen was forcibly removed from my possession, which put an end to my scribbling of notes and
meant that, for the remainder of my stay in Siglo XXI,
I would find myself constantly reaching for it only to
be reminded that it was not there—and that my right
arm might as well have been amputated after all. Having
already resigned myself during the bracelet episode to
the idea that my world was over, I mumbled that I was
a journalist, which elicited the almost-enthusiastic
response from Migra 4: "Are you famous?" She was less
enthused, however, at the suggestion that she google
my name to determine the answer, and, from then on
out, I had to rely mainly on my memory—which had
at least more or less recovered from that morning's wine
overdose—rather than a writing utensil to preserve the
details of my detention.

The next day, I would succeed in getting my hands
on the only pen inside the facility, which was attached

to the wall and was usually in perennial use as detainees signed and re-signed their names to an infinite rotation of stapled paper lists certifying their existence in a system that strips existence of all meaning—such being the nature of arbitrary and bureaucratic power and the need to exert control over dehumanized bodies. There was a list for every mealtime, a list for phone calls, a list to confirm that you had received your toiletry package with deodorant and sanitary napkins. My efforts to frenetically channel through the dilapidated Bic as many thoughts as I could think of would first be interrupted by another detainee, who wanted to know what list I was signing, and then fully thwarted when the pen ceased to function. The dearth of ink would not put a stop to the stapled paper list rotation, and the signature-signing process simply became more of a signature-engraving process, with inkless pen tip as engraving tool.

During my induction into Siglo XXI, additional precautionary measures carried out by the policewomen included removing the pads from all my sports bras and bathing suit tops, which would create hours of fun for me when I had to reinstate them later. Once everything had been thoroughly examined, it was all placed back in the bags—minus the spare T-shirt, pair of panties, and smattering of other crucial items I was permitted to take into jail with me, such as my passport, my notebook (perhaps to enhance the torment of not having a pen), my packet of cranberries, and my Palestinian olive oil soap. After some debate, I was also permitted to take the bread and slab of Manchego cheese from Walmart, although the plastic bag containing the bread first had to be trimmed with scissors so that there was as little plastic involved as possible. The long, green, black-seeded fruit gifted to me by Alejandra—and alternately called *paterna, cuajinicuil, chalahuite*, and who knows what else— was cleared for entry, as well, completing the medley of objects that now constituted my identity.

Migra 4 ordered me to stand up and collect my bags, which were to be deposited in a room across the hall that was already teeming with bags of all sizes and colors. Each had been affixed with a white slip denoting the country of origin of the bag's owner along with a number. In the case of my two slips, the word CONGO had been crossed out in purple marker and replaced with ESTADOS UNIDOS, also in purple marker, and the numbers 123 and 129, respectively. I wedged my duffel bag and backpack into a corner and, preparing myself for the moment of truth, asked Migra 4 if everyone would be wearing face masks inside. She winked at me: "You can wear yours"—a reassuring arrangement, no doubt, as Mexico had just entered its third coronavirus wave and was holding steady on the shortlist of countries with most COVID deaths worldwide.

I was led down the hallway to the heavy metal door that would convey me into the innards of the twenty-first century. There I was frisked by another female guard, who energetically pinched the cups of my bra and whose objections to the now-reduced size of the plastic bag with bread were overridden by the other gatekeepers. To one side was a stack of thin grey mattresses and a stack of thin blankets; I was instructed to pick up one of each. The door opened, and I was engulfed in an extraordinary multilingual din that evoked a severely overcrowded school cafeteria or locker room. Among the hundreds of faces in front of me, there was not a single face mask in sight, although there was plenty of coughing. I forced myself to breathe into my own mask while smiling an apologetic smile that no one could see and stepping gingerly through the crowd clutching my mattress, blanket, *paterna-cuajinicuil-chalahuite*, and other accessories. An out-of-body experience ensued in which I was able to observe myself as a caricature of gringo awkwardness and general uncoolness, with nothing but privilege to cling to as I navigated a mass of bodies that— even in their transitory state as migrants—exuded more permanence and assuredness of being than the person whose country was largely responsible for putting them there. Migra 4, who had also entered the maelstrom to perform the requisite perfunctory imposition of order, bellowed at me to find a space for my mattress—the problem being that there was no space.

The layout of the place is as follows: the door opens into a large room full of concrete tables, which are used for eating, sleeping, and slumping over in despair. Hanging from the ceiling is a television set, from which it is sometimes possible to glean the hour of the day— otherwise, you have to ask the guards. During the daytime, mattresses and blankets line the walls; at night, they proliferate across the floor, rendering the room impassable. Also lining the walls are posters with instructions in several languages as to how to—allegedly—go about requesting asylum and other rights, although the lack of cooperativeness on the part of the jailkeepers re: basically any and every query from inmates means that the signage ultimately serves more of a decorative function. "*Más tarde*" (later) is the preferred response by Inami officials to existential and mundane questions alike: "When can I meet with someone to discuss my case?"; "When will I know if I'm being deported?"; "When can I have a book to read?" In the event that an Inami official does not feel like pronouncing the words "*más tarde*," a shrug also suffices, as does silence.

To your right as you enter is the counter where the lists are placed and the wall to which the pen is attached. This is also where meals are served, through a gap in the slatted screen dividing the counter from a small office that can only be entered from the hallway outside the metal jail door. The screen appears specially designed to induce vertigo—at least in my own experience of spending extended periods of time staring at it while waiting for Inami or other officials to wander into the office such that they might be imploringly appealed to via the gap and have more opportunities to say "*más tarde*."

To your left as you enter, meanwhile, is a corridor lined with more mattresses, blankets, and women atop them in assorted physical manifestations of limbo. Off of the corridor are various rooms with more of the same plus toilets with no doors, and at the end is a room with curtainless showers and a laundry area. The door to the prison yard, finally, is located just opposite the entrance, and is locked at night. In the morning, a line forms in front of the door in anticipation of it being unlocked—by which time the line has become a teeming throng of flesh against flesh that bursts forth into the yard in a momentary approximation of liberation, accompanied by cheers. After the race to collect the fruit that has fallen from the mango tree, you can sit in the flea-infested grass or on the sports court with a single deflated ball and revel in the feeling of being monitored by police from beyond the towering fence. The grass is also used for drying laundry, while the tree is an apparent source of empowerment and/or consolation to the detainees who can be seen embracing its trunk.

It was in the prison yard that I had my first real human interaction in Siglo XXI. Migra 4 had interrupted my fruitless search for a spot to place my mattress by threateningly notifying me that I had best line up for dinner while there was dinner to be had. I folded my mattress with belongings inside, as everyone else had done, and placed it on top of another one for the time being. I cannot recall any of the food I consumed in the detention center aside from the Walmart bread (the Manchego cheese ended up in the trash due to lack of refrigeration), but my notes relate that the meals consisted of tortillas, rice and beans, and chicken with vegetables. According to many detainees, vomiting was a regular side effect of eating in Siglo XXI; according to the Cubans, the chicken should have been fried and not boiled. And it was a contingent of Cubans who made up my welcoming committee of sorts, approaching me under the concrete overhang outside where my tray of food and I had sought refuge from the incipient rain as women scrambled to collect their laundry from the grass.

Gathering around, the Cubans announced that they did not want me to feel alone and asked me to identify my national origins. Once the riotous laughter at my response had subsided, I volunteered that I had relatives on my father's side in Cuba, as though this somehow made me slightly less ridiculous. The relatives lived in the town of Jiguaní in the province of Granma, I babbled, and I had visited them in 2006. One of the Cuban detainees nodded in confirmation of Jiguaní's existence; another one wanted to know, based on my perennial sunburn, if the *migra* had been picking up people on the beach, and yet another opined that, as it was Sunday, the *migra* had been bored and just wanted to fuck with people. The Cubans were thoroughly offended on my behalf that the Mexicans had dared to apprehend an American, to whom borders were not meant to apply— even as some of them told me how they had traversed no fewer than fourteen countries to reach Mexico from Cuba, including the notorious corpse-ridden Darién Gap between Panama and Colombia.

Migra 6, whom I had not yet met, would later complain to me that the Cubans of Siglo XXI were a constant headache: loud, ornery, and in possession of a frequently unintelligible manner of speaking, as they insisted on "eating their words." For me, on the other hand, they quickly came to embody defiant resilience, particularly given their habit of bursting into song. Often, these songs were improvised—and pretty much any event could be the topic for spontaneous musical verse accompanied by handclapping and hip movement. Say, for example, a detainee managed to corner an Inami agent to inquire about the next authorized visit to her husband in the men's section of the prison—which by all accounts was even more horrifically overcrowded and where the jailers were more prone to physical abuse. Rather than simply report the upshot of the inquiry to her companions, she might produce a short rhythmic tune about the back-and-forth and being told she could see her husband "*más tarde*." One female Cuban detainee, members of my welcoming committee reported, had devised a song with upbeat clapping that went: "Let the mango fall!"—which sounded much sexier in Spanish, and which was sung underneath the tree in the prison yard. The Cubans swore by the song's effectiveness.

The Cubans and I were, you might say, in exactly opposite boats. While they were trying desperately to reach my disagreeable homeland—a land that was nonetheless to thank for the passport that had until now enabled me to gallivant about the world with minimal difficulty—I was concerned that being deported to the U.S. would disrupt my upcoming trip to Havana. For months, I had been determined to be injected with one of Cuba's homegrown coronavirus vaccines. However, flights to the island from Mexico had been temporarily suspended due to the pandemic, requiring Cuba-bound travelers to make rounds of assorted European, South American, and other airports. In my case, I was scheduled to fly in August to Istanbul, my first transatlantic trip since 2019, where I would then catch a plane to Havana—a circuitous route, no doubt, but nothing compared to trekking through fourteen countries and encountering corpses in the Darién. Call it first-world travel problems.

Most of the Cuban detainees I spoke to in Siglo XXI cited shortages on the island—of food, medicine, electricity—as the impetus for their departure. By chance, July 11, the day of my imprisonment, was the very day that protests briefly erupted in Cuba over a lack of basic necessities. The bloodthirsty Cuban exile crowd in Miami and its allies in U.S. media outlets—nostalgic for the good old days of Fulgencio Batista's brutal dictatorship—tripped over themselves demanding U.S.

intervention, as though a sixty-year blockade had not been intervention enough.

Indeed, lost in the right-wing narrative on Cuba is the ostensibly glaringly obvious fact that embargoes cause shortages—and that a country that prevents the Cuban medical establishment from obtaining syringes during a pandemic should not be tasked with saving Cuba. For an illustration of the criminally lethal nature of such coercive economic measures, one need look no further than the 1996 response by then U.S. ambassador to the United Nations Madeleine Albright to the estimate that half a million Iraqi children had thus far died on account of U.S. sanctions: "We think the price is worth it." Leave it to capitalism to issue a positive cost-benefit analysis of the indirect mass slaughter of kids.

For more than six decades, the United States has sought to destroy the Cuban example and to thereby disabuse other populations of the treacherous notion that such things as healthcare and education should be free. Any and all Cuban shortcomings are cast as evidence of the inevitable failure of anti-capitalist systems rather than effects of the asphyxiating blockade under which the island has been forced to operate. Cuba's internationally celebrated medical diplomacy program, which has succeeded in the face of the blockade and has seen tens of thousands of medics deployed across the globe to the general benefit of humanity, is regularly decried as slavery by the *Wall Street Journal*'s Mary Anastasia O'Grady, Brazilian President Jair Bolsonaro, and other preposterous folk.

True to form, the United States was quickly up in arms over the Cuban government's security crackdown in response to the July 11 demonstrations. But it bears underscoring that, while critiquing Cuba for jailing dissidents and committing human rights violations is not in itself an invalid undertaking, these critiques would surely command more moral traction were the U.S. not embroiled in far more comprehensive human rights abuses than Cuba. This would especially be the case were the U.S. not continuing to preside over an illegal prison on Cuban territory in Guantánamo Bay, where inmates had been subjected to "sodomy" (the official euphemism is "rectal rehydration," although it is debatable whether this even sounds better) and where "waterboarding of detainees was so gruesome that even CIA officials wept," according to the *Los Angeles Times*.

Online, a number of images purporting to depict the unrest in Cuba were revealed to have been appropriated from coverage of events as diverse as the 2011 protests in Egypt, a July 2021 celebration in Buenos Aires following the Argentine soccer team's victory in the Copa América, and even a 2018 May Day parade in Havana itself. The Biden administration soon decided to out-Trump Trump, who had imposed 243 additional sanctions on Cuba, by imposing even more—which naturally only promised to further aggravate the Cuban situation in what amounted to an ongoing act of war by the U.S. Then again, aggravation had long been the point.

In January 1960, one year after the triumph of the Cuban Revolution, U.S. President Dwight Eisenhower had proposed a neat resolution to the problem of Fidel Castro during a White House conference. As per the writeup of the conference that appears on the State Department website, "the President said that. . . we could quarantine Cuba. If they (the Cuban people) are hungry, they will throw Castro out." And *voilà*, the old democracy-by-famine trick! A few months later, in April, Eisenhower's deputy assistant secretary of state for inter-American affairs Lester Mallory produced a similarly charming memorandum, in which the very first "salient consideration" was that "the majority of Cubans support Castro." It followed that "every possible means should be undertaken promptly to weaken the economic life of Cuba." Lots more words were then deployed in order to suggest that this was actually civilized business rather than savagery: "If such a policy is adopted, it should be the result of a positive decision which would call forth a line of action which, while as adroit and inconspicuous as possible, makes the greatest inroads in denying money and supplies to Cuba, to decrease monetary and real wages, to bring about hunger, desperation and overthrow of government." After all, there is nothing quite like adroit and inconspicuous starvation.

In February of 1962, the grand "Embargo on All Trade with Cuba" entered into effect under the supervision of John F. Kennedy, who had taken care beforehand to stockpile for himself no fewer than 1,200 Cuban cigars. All sales of medicine and food were banned under what is still the most exhaustive embargo ever imposed on any country by the U.S. and, while the sanctions regime has undergone a multitude of cosmetic adjustments over the decades, doing business with Cuba remains such a colossal pain in the ass—with potentially gargantuan legal and financial repercussions for guilty parties—that it all seems anything but "adroit and inconspicuous."

When I finally made it to Havana in February 2022—following numerous postponements of my trip but just in time for the sixty-year anniversary of the embargo—basic goods like milk and coffee were con-spicuously absent. I was, however, able to receive the Cuban-made Soberana Plus COVID vaccine booster no problem, and Cuba continued to put the rest of the world to shame in terms of vaccine production and adminis-tration. Over the course of my month-long stay in the country, I would speak with more than one Cuban who had already tried out life in the U.S. and opted to return home. Cuba had its problems, for sure, I was told—but it was at least better than the American nightmare to the north. The United States, for its part, persists in its conviction that it has all the time in the world to van-quish Cuba. And, hey, if regime change doesn't pan out, Cubans can still starve in the meantime.

In Havana I would also make the acquaintance of a forty-three-year-old man named Eraudis, in front of whom I gracefully crashed while jogging one morning on the Malecón, where he sat perched atop the seawall just next to the plaque specifying that the seaside prom-enade had been constructed in 1901 under the auspices of "Leonard Wood, U.S.A.," former chief of staff of the U.S. military, governor general of the Philippines, and military governor of the island of Cuba. Both of Eraudis' legs had been blown off by a land mine outside the U.S. base in Guantánamo when he was performing his own military service at the age of nineteen; he now moved about with one makeshift prosthetic leg and a pair of crutches, and apologized that he could not carry me home. Sending me on my way with instructions on what to do about my grazed knees and palms (apply soap and water and calm down), Eraudis would monitor the healing process over the coming days during our matutinal encounters on the Malecón, where I now paid close attention to holes in the ground. One morning, he prescribed an additional treatment of seawater, and sent his companion—himself a musician-fisherman who was partaking of some breakfast rum—to fill a couple of bottles on the rocks beyond the seawall. Eraudis' father, it turned out, had died of COVID at his home in Guantánamo province at the start of the pandemic. His voice choking up, he noted that he needed to phone his mother to see if she had gone to the cemetery that week. And then he told me that, all things considered, he felt lucky because "there is always someone worse off than you."

As for my Cuban interlocutors in Siglo XXI, they of course could not be expected to give me the entire historical background to their own plight, complete with a review of imperial contributions to public misery and quotes from Lester Mallory. Rather, they offered

the condensed, immediate version of events: there were
shortages on the island, and so they left. When I was
able to wrest hold of the prison pen for a few moments,
I scribbled in my notebook: "Cubans say no one leaves
their country and walks thru selva for a week if they
don't have to" (*selva* meaning jungle). One Cuban
woman remarked that the walking part was not actually so bad because at least you were focused on moving
in a forward direction and surviving in general—which
was more than could be said for the Siglo XXI experience, where the future had been put indefinitely on hold
and the lack of motion allowed your trauma to catch up
with you. Things were not helped, I was told, by the
tendency of a certain Mexico-based Cuban diplomatic
representative to hang up on people who were trying to
sort out their next step after jail.

Daniely, a Cuban in her twenties who forcibly
adopted me as her mattress-mate, would later comment
with her signature spiritedness as she threaded another
inmate's eyebrows: "We are not terrorists or criminals,
we are just people who left our homes out of necessity."
(Perhaps also out of necessity, Biden had gone ahead and
left the tiny island on the State Sponsors of Terrorism
List to which it had been unceremoniously added by
the outgoing Trump.) The forcible adoption by Daniely

had come about when, after my arrival dinner, I had confirmed that the only available space for my mattress was directly in front of the toilet—whereas Daniely's spot was a full few meters away. Dragging me over to it by the hand while scolding me for wearing a face mask ("Will you take that fucking thing off I feel like I can't breathe"), she thrust some spare clothes at me for use as a pillow and silenced my meek objections that my presence on half of the mattress would cause her discomfort: "Here we share everything." In the end, it was enormously comforting to have two Cuban feet in my face all night—even as I tried to distance my own feet from her face by sliding them from the mattress onto the floor. When she perceived the sliding mid-slumber, she grabbed my feet and plunked them back on her make-shift pillow, which consisted of various pairs of socks.

5: SOLIDARITY

With dyed blonde cornrows and a long gray curve-accentuating dress, Daniely made me feel even guiltier about my slovenly appearance, clad as I was in disintegrating black running shorts and a disintegrating red tank top. After all, I was not the one who had been trekking through the jungle for weeks. There were no mirrors in the twenty-first-century prison, and I was particularly relieved to learn of Daniely's threading abilities after discovering during my allotted visit to the luggage room for a change of clothes that my tweezers had been confiscated from my duffel bag, never to be returned—which meant that being deported to the U.S. with a beard and mustache had been temporarily added to my inventory of preoccupations.

At one end of Daniely's mattress was a pile of mangoes, tortillas, and other items she was saving for her husband, who, detained in the men's section of Siglo XXI, had determined that Cuba was not the only place suffering from a scarcity of food. When I asked her what the deal was with telephone calls—which Migra 4 had sworn to me would happen "*más tarde*"—Daniely winked at me: "What, you've never been in jail? You get one phone call." Only once during my twenty-first-century detention would I see Daniely's energy levels languish—a moment recorded in my notebook as: "Daniely is bored." She had just broadcast her boredom to another Cuban woman, who had suggested that she read a book if the prison library ever amended its opening hours from "*más tarde*" to something more tangible. This woman had somehow finagled herself a copy of Dante's *Inferno* in Spanish, which seemed to be fitting reading material.

Moment of boredom aside, Daniely could usually be seen braiding the hair of other detainees, dispensing with incoming unibrows, or cracking jokes to anyone who needed to be jolted out of despair—like the sobbing Honduran woman in a red dress who lay contorted on a clump of mattresses at the end of the hallway next to the showers. I had also ended up on this clump at some point on the elusive timeline that stretched from the moment I was intercepted by the Cubans at dinner and the moment I ostensibly "went to bed"—this being easier than saying "reclined on Daniely's spare T-shirt under a light that had been dimmed to slightly-less-than-glaring mode as three Guatemalan women conducted a prayer ceremony on top of me and hacking coughs echoed throughout the room."

Had I been left to my own devices in Siglo XXI, I would have spent far more time alone—trapped in the prison-within-a-prison of my mind. However, while I can certainly say that I do now understand why they confiscate your shoelaces, I can also say I was preemptively yanked back from any potentially catastrophic mental precipice by the very human companionship and conversation that, nonsensically enough, I initially recoiled at—convinced as I was that it was preferable to wallow in my misery and think vicious thoughts about the system. In reality, the emotional solidarity that I received was itself an anti-systemic fuck you to U.S.-backed policies playing out on migrant bodies.

This was the case, for example, when I was torn away from plodding methodically around the outdoor sports court—executing a dramatically morose turn at each corner—by a group seated on the court's concrete floor and comprising Honduran, Salvadoran, Venezuelan, Nicaraguan, and Cuban women, who in a staggered chorus of purposefully exaggerated English shouted: "Hello my friend!" Refusing to hear my excuses for needing to continue to plod, they patted the concrete next to them: "Sit."

It was the case, too, with Kimberly, the young woman who had fled Honduras after her two sisters were killed and who rescued me not once but twice from debilitating solitude—first when I was endeavoring to fuse myself with the wall in front of the toilets while forcing bits of hardened Walmart bread into my mouth and second when I had resigned myself to consumption by fleas in the grass, where I assumed a cross-legged position while listening to the chatter of the armed guards beyond the fence and mentally transporting myself to other, greener grasses. On both occasions, Kimberly greeted me with the question: "Why are you alone?" In the bathroom, she accepted a chunk of bread and broke off a piece for another Honduran; on the grass, she spread out her Siglo XXI blanket for us to sit on. Pudgy, wearing a short flowery dress, and with a perpetual twinkle in her eye, Kimberly asked me to teach her the English words for things like "love" and "Kimberly." Giggling, she suggested that maybe I could adopt her.

In the case of the clump of mattresses by the showers, meanwhile, I had been snagged by Daniely and the others sitting with the sobbing Honduran in the red dress as I went about pacing to the extent that is possible in a corridor jam-packed with bodies with nowhere to go, the door to outside having already been locked. My attempted feigning of having some place to be was roundly dismissed, and I assumed a position at the edge of the clump in time to hear Daniely remark with a mischievous smirk: "If this is the twenty-first century, I'd hate to see the twenty-second."

The Honduran, it was explained to me, missed her children in Honduras and had been unable to reach them by phone for several days. I never did learn her name, just as I never learned the names of most of the women I met behind bars—who themselves mostly referred to me as "Estados Unidos," just as they referred to the lone Chinese detainee as "China" and the Bangladeshi as "Bangladesh." In retrospect, I would struggle with feelings of guilt over my failure to record names—as though I were erasing identity and agency and simply perpetuating the mainstream perception of a dehumanized blob of migrants. But while I may not have been equipped for a Siglo XXI roll call, I did wield a surplus of other biographical details that had bombarded me from all directions.

For instance, I did not know the name of the forty-something-year-old Cuban lady who had spent the past twenty-eight days in Siglo XXI and diagnosed herself as "probably already traumatized," but I did know that she had traveled from Cuba to Uruguay and then all the way up to the Guatemala-Mexico border.

There she and her husband had paid a coyote four thousand Mexican pesos (approximately two hundred U.S.
dollars) for some portion of the onward trajectory, and
were promptly relieved of all the rest of their money,
as well—along with passports, cell phones, and changes
of clothing—and deposited on the side of the road for
easy pickup by the *migra*. I promised myself that, if I ever
made it back to Zipolite, I would never again throw a fit
when a dog barked in the middle of the night or the egg-
shell did not perfectly separate itself from the hardboiled
egg without taking bits of egg white along with it.

Nor did I know the name of the thirty-something-
year-old Honduran whose father had been killed in
Honduras, and who joked at one point to Kimberly—
herself a lesbian—that Siglo XXI might yet turn her
into a lesbian as well. Such a conversion, the woman
whose father had been killed reckoned, could be practical not only in situations of indefinite all-female detention but in life in general. I did not even know the name
of the twenty-year-old bespectacled Honduran in slacks
and cardigan, who like Daniely made me feel horribly
underdressed for jail and who held her towel up for me
in lieu of a shower curtain. I did, however, know that
she had studied human rights at university—an ironic
subject in Honduras and Siglo XXI alike.

The human rights student formed part of the group that disrupted my plodding around the sports court. Lying on the concrete with her head in a Cuban lap, she had been listening to the others recount tales from the Darién Gap, which Honduran migrants did not have to traverse as part of their northward journeys— although they were naturally still prey to gangs, thieves, soldiers, and all manner of other existence-imperiling phenomena. As per *The Manual* website—which purports to "show men how to live a life that is more engaged. Whether it be fashion, food, drink, travel, grooming, or the outdoors, we bring authenticity and understanding to it all"—the Darién Gap is sixty-six miles of "one of the world's most dangerous jungles," and is famous for "Things that will kill you." Dangers include the fer-de-lance pit viper, the Brazilian wandering spider, the black scorpion, the spiked Chunga palm tree, botflies, drug traffickers, guerrillas belonging to the Revolutionary Armed Forces of Colombia, and unexploded ordnance dating from the Cold War, when everyone's favorite communist-fighting superpower "ran training runs, dropping bombs over the jungle."

But if you're an undocumented migrant rather than a man seeking authentic engagement with the universe, the Brazilian wandering spider is perhaps the least of your worries. The Cubans and Venezuelans in the sports court group compared notes from their respective treks through the treacherous stretch: the people they had known who had gone in one side and never come out the other, the thirteen-year-old girl who had been raped multiple times along the way, the need to keep moving even as you passed cadavers—each of which effectively served as a reminder of the very short distance between life and death for those relegated by the international capitalist order to the inferior echelons of humankind.

When you ran out of food and water, of course, it was all the more important to keep moving. And, as in Siglo XXI, there were plenty of chances to display the solidarity that capitalism would never achieve—indeed, that it had labored so hard to destroy—even as migrants trudged north in the direction of the very epicenter of capitalist destruction that many viewed as their only present option for salvation. One Cuban, recalling an episode in a Darién ravine in which some of her countrymen had intervened to save other migrants from becoming cadavers themselves, declared: "Say what you will about our manners, but at the end of the day *el hombre cubano es muy humanitario*." The conversation then turned to me and my plight of not wanting to be put on an airplane and sent direct to the U.S. in an air-conditioned cabin without having to confront rapists or fer-de-lance pit vipers.

Squirming, I presented my usual arguments for avoiding the homeland—"I don't like it"; "It's scary and disconnected from humanity"; "There is no life there"—which were no doubt compelling to people running for their lives, and were processed with a mix of amusement, bewilderment, and apparent concern for my soundness of mind. I had just started to feel like an incurably ludicrous asshole when the conversation shifted once again, this time to the shower facilities of the twenty-first century and specifically the fact that I had yet to experience them. The Honduran human rights student, raising her head from the Cuban lap in which it had been resting, offered to show me the ropes—and off the sports court we went into the teeming room with concrete tables, one of which was occupied by the Chinese detainee and two Cubans who had undertaken to teach her such critical Spanish vocabulary as "shorts." As she spoke no English either, her interpersonal communications were severely restricted, but detainees and Inami officials alike told me she had been there a long, long time.

The student, who was practically half my age and exuded an air of serenity amidst the chaos, guided me down the corridor to the showers, pausing at her mattress along the way to retrieve a blue towel and at my mattress to retrieve my soap ("It's from Palestine," I offered helpfully). Once in the shower room, she ushered me into the stall that was farthest to the left, instructed me on how to manipulate the faucet and where to place my clothes, and diligently held her towel up—not that it really mattered if anyone saw me naked, but I appreciated the symbolic rejection of total surveillance and the fleeting recuperation of a semblance of privacy, especially in light of the presence of a uniformed Inami official overseeing shower operations and emitting power over bare migrant flesh.

My minute-and-a-half of alone time with the Palestinian soap gave me the chance to review past instances when I had been on the receiving end of inordinate generosity from folks the United States had fucked over. Lebanon came to mind, where my Polish friend Amelia and I had conducted a two-month hitchhiking tour in 2006 in which much ground had been covered more than once on account of the country's diminutive size. Much ground was also not coverable, given that it had recently been blown to bits in the July War, a thirty-four-day assault by the Israeli military that killed some 1,200 people, primarily civilians. The George W. Bush administration had abetted the pulverization of roads, bridges, neighborhoods, and humans by rush-shipping precision guided bombs to Israel—a shipment that, the *New York Times* reported on July 22, had "not been announced publicly. . . But one American official said normal procedures usually do not include rushing deliveries within days of a request." The U.S. had also maneuvered repeatedly to delay a ceasefire so as to allow Israel to do for as long as possible what it does best: terrorize people in the name of fighting terror.

For two months, Amelia and I had been picked up, driven around at high speeds (in keeping with the unofficial Lebanese national mantra that it takes only five minutes to get from the mountains to the sea), over-fed, plied with Lebanese wine, and taken olive-picking, Roman-ruin-hopping, hiking, swimming, dancing, rifle-shooting, unexploded-cluster-bomb-viewing, and giant-crater-exploring where apartment buildings had previously stood. Not once did we pay for accommodations—or anything else, for that matter—as there was rarely a person who picked us up hitchhiking and did not invite us to stay the night at their home or even move in with them if we so desired. Our catalogue of hosts included people who had lost family members, friends, and possessions to aerial bombardment. It also included Palestinian refugees, who thanks to more than seven decades of ethnic cleansing operations by the United States' favorite regional partner in crime found themselves under Israeli attack in Lebanon rather than in Palestine. Amelia and I were continuously bombarded with gifts, and had to hitchhike back to Turkey with an array of bags and an enormous wall clock featuring the Hezbollah logo.

The more I thought about it in the Siglo XXI shower, the more it seemed I had in fact spent most of my contemporary life being treated very well by people my country had treated very badly—from Colombian peasants terrorized by a fervently United States-backed right-wing state fond of massacring civilians on behalf of elite economic tyranny to Salvadorans terrorized by pretty much the same thing. Iranians of the Axis of Evil, Syrians of the expanded Axis of Evil, and the Mexican "rapists" Trump had determined were inhabiting the most proximate section of the U.S. Backyard had welcomed me with relentless hospitality unmerited by an imperial emissary—and yet my treatment as a human being by those whose dehumanization underpinned imperial conquest only further demonstrated how the whole arrangement sucked. Granted, my treatment at the hands of Inami personnel did not technically qualify as the most hospitable reception ever, but it was without doubt superior to the reception accorded "illegal" visitors to the United States and was also ultimately a result of U.S. handiwork anyway; as my friend Diego in Tapachula would later observe with regard to my imprisonment: "You're like the gringa collateral damage of U.S. policies."

To be sure, "Siglo XXI" is a not inappropriate name for a human-rights-deficient, abuse-friendly "migration station" in a twenty-first century in which much of the earth's population is essentially imprisoned in U.S.-inflicted political and economic nightmares—and often forced to migrate because of them. And as if the irony were not already sufficiently cruel, a Mexican senator from AMLO's party, MORENA, had in April 2021 proposed amending the "migration station" label to "center for humanitarian protection of migrating persons."

Completing my shower, I exited the protective shield furnished by the human rights student, who had offered what hospitality she could in a place where no one was at home and who now escorted me to the laundry area so that I could wash the disintegrating red tank top, which had been replaced with my pink tank top from Barcelona that said "Barcelona" and featured butterflies and Gaudí's Sagrada Familia. Although I was not usually inclined to purchase such items, I had been immediately won over by its perfect degree of cheesiness upon glimpsing it outside a souvenir shop a few years earlier—when my parents were still living in the city and had yet to be afflicted by the pandemic-induced lapse in judgment that caused them to return to the homeland. I passed the shop on my regular walks from their apartment near the Arc de Triomf to the sea, a trajectory that now seemed almost mystical in my recollection, as did all trajectories that did not involve being imprisoned.

When I asked the human rights student how things were going these days in Honduras, she just smiled a half-smile and wordlessly shook her head. It was a stupid question—sort of like asking someone submerged in a vat of boiling bleach how they are doing. The June 2009 coup d'état against Manuel Zelaya, which had transpired approximately half the student's lifetime ago and had been tirelessly legitimized by the Barack Obama administration, had set the stage for an ongoing bloodbath—but at least Honduras had been rescued from Zelaya, who had done such diabolical things as raise the minimum wage. In other heretical behavior, the slightly left-curious Zelaya had pursued agrarian reform benefitting peasant farmers and had opted to consult impoverished communities whose territories had been usurped by toxic corporate mining endeavors on how they felt about the whole setup. It was no accident that the motto of the right-wing post-coup regime was "Honduras is Open for Business."

As for the business of killing in Honduras, post-coup violence by the state—including assassinations, torture, and forced disappearances—targeted members of the anti-coup resistance, journalists, teachers, human rights and environmental defenders, campesinos, LGBT+ activists, and others objecting to the general neoliberal free-for-all that swiftly obliterated hopes of a less unequal society. Concern for any aspect of justice in the country became an ever more dangerous business, and death squads emerged in the Honduran security forces—lest anyone was not yet suffering flashbacks to the 1980s, when the nation had been dubbed the "U.S.S. Honduras" in reference to its service as a launchpad for the "large-scale terrorist war" (description courtesy of Noam Chomsky) against neighboring Nicaragua by U.S.-backed Contra mercenaries.

During this eventful stretch of the Cold War, Hondurans had been kept in line and discouraged from following in Nicaraguan footsteps—which had strayed dangerously from the straight and narrow path of United States control—with the help of Battalion 316, the

CIA-trained death squad that, as the *Baltimore Sun* recalls, "terrorized Honduras for much of the 1980s." Speaking to Telesur in 2015, anthropologist and Honduras expert Adrienne Pine reflected on the exploits of Battalion 316, which had "laid the groundwork for the implementation of U.S.-led neoliberal economic policies, of which the Honduran military itself was a primary beneficiary." Drawing parallels with the present day, Pine credited a combination of factors with enabling the "neoliberal plunder of the country currently underway": on the one hand, "pro-democracy" programs funded by the ever-friendly U.S. Agency for International Development (USAID) and the National Endowment for Democracy (NED) and, on the other, death squads within the police, military, and military police.

Fast-forward to 2019, the tenth anniversary of the coup, and the situation had hardly improved. In an email to me that May, Dana Frank—professor emerita at the University of California, Santa Cruz and author of *The Long Honduran Night: Resistance, Terror, and the United States in the Aftermath of the Coup*—commented on the "escalating repression of the opposition by Honduran security forces." This repression served in part, she said, "to silence those who challenge the U.S. military presence in Honduras and the region, who challenge illegal

mining and dam projects that serve transnational corporate interests, who defend labor rights, and who seek
to build a future in which Honduras is sovereign and
independent of U.S. domination."

In keeping with the logic of imperial domination,
U.S. aid to homicide-happy Honduran security forces
had increased after the coup, and the further prolifer-
ation of U.S. military bases in the country meant that
the U.S.S. Honduras was, for all intents and purposes,
back in business. And just as the Cold War had provided
plenty of opportunities for politically expedient U.S.
collaboration with drug traffickers, the post-coup pan-
orama was a fine backdrop for drug war hypocrisy. In
the Aguán Valley in northeastern Honduras, elite land-
owners allied with the coup regime waged a particularly vicious war on small farmers seeking to assert their
land rights. As Frank writes in *The Long Honduran Night*,
"security guards and others allegedly working for"
the likes of (since deceased) biofuels magnate Miguel
Facussé "hunted down campesinos like animals up and
down the roads, rivers, and pathways of the valley." It so
happens that these guards also worked in close conjunction with Honduran security forces on the receiving end
of United States drug war funds—despite the fact that
Facussé was a cocaine importer, which the U.S. had been

aware of since at least 2004, according to WikiLeaked cables. Frank summarizes the nefarious upshot:

"Precisely as US funding for the Honduran military and police escalated under the pretext of fighting the drug war, then, US-supported troops were conducting joint operations with the security guards of someone the United Sates knew was a drug trafficker, in order to violently repress a campesino movement on behalf of his illegal claims to vast swaths of the Aguán Valley."

The coup paved the way for all sorts of other illegal stuff, too—like the charter city scheme that sprung forth from the brain of U.S. economist Paul Romer, who had concluded that it would be a nifty experiment to erect a bunch of privatized city-states on other people's land. Basically, the charter cities would be exempt from domestic Honduran laws and governed instead by investors. This glorious premise caused the *Wall Street Journal*'s aforementioned Mary Anastasia O'Grady of Cuban medical "slave trade" fame to ejaculate all over the paper's pages about how "the little country that stood up to the world to defend its democracy seems to be affirming a belief that it needs to change if it wants to ward off future assaults on freedom."

In O'Grady-land, of course, defending one's democracy means overthrowing one's democratically elected president to attain "freedom"—but not freedom for people. Writing from the Honduran capital of Tegucigalpa on Valentine's Day, 2011, O'Grady gushed with passion: "What advocate of free markets hasn't, at one time or another, fantasized about running away to a desert island to start a country where economic liberty would be the law of the land?" A couple of points in response: First of all, Honduras is not a desert island but rather a very inhabited territory whose residents have already experienced colonialism and suffered accordingly—for more than five centuries. Second of all, contemporary runaway economic fantasies have presumably been sufficiently fulfilled by, like, the Honduran sweatshop industry— which reached peak notoriety in the mid-'90s with the news that celebrity television personality Kathie Lee Gifford was making bank off of clothing manufactured in slavery-like conditions (the *New York Times*' Larry Rohter assured critics that Hondurans making less than forty cents an hour still thought this was "the surest road to a better life"). Third of all, you know O'Grady is bad when even Jeffrey Goldberg—the editor-in-chief of *The Atlantic* who is not himself known for skimping on imperial propaganda—once began a dispatch: "If I didn't know better, I would say that Mary Anastasia O'Grady, the *Wall Street Journal* polemicist who never met a fascist Central American oligarch she didn't like, is preparing to invade the Bay of Pigs all over again."

It's not just Central America and Cuba, of course. O'Grady has also bestowed the honor of "The Man Who Saved Colombia" upon former right-wing president-cum-war criminal and devoted U.S. buddy Álvaro Uribe, who "salvaged democracy" by, inter alia, presiding over the slaughter of peasants. Uribe, incidentally, was in attendance at the post-coup "Honduras is Open for Business" conference in 2011 that boasted the participation of charter-city king Romer himself, in addition to assorted U.S. government officials, investors from fifty-five different countries, and the planet's then-richest individual, Carlos Slim. Curiously, O'Grady's celebrated preventive measures against "future assaults on freedom" in Honduras—with "freedom" entailing the auctioning off of national territory to corporate sponsors—required altering the Honduran constitution, which was the very crime Zelaya was accused of plotting and that was invoked to justify his ("democratic") overthrow.

As the powers that be spun it, Zelaya had sought to extend his time in power beyond the single constitutionally permitted term by suggesting that maybe the Honduran citizenry would like to vote about the possibility of amending portions of the document in question, which hailed from the heyday of the U.S.S. Honduras and entrenched the "fascist oligarch" version of democracy. In reality, the suggested vote would have taken place at the same November 2009 elections in which Zelaya was already categorically ineligible to run, thus derailing the *golpista* argument that he was maneuvering to remain president for eternity. But desperate times call for a suspension of logic, and so off Zelaya went, in the wee hours of June 28, to Costa Rica— still in his pajamas and escorted by members of the Honduran military. Honduras' constitutional one-term limit has since been eliminated, but since it was done to allow for the reelection of far-right narco-dictator Juan Orlando Hernández it was totally fine.

I myself spent a segment of the coup's aftermath in Honduras, arriving exactly one month after Zelaya's ouster to Tegucigalpa, where I would remain until December—minus a couple of intra-Honduran road trips, a jaunt to Nicaragua, and a forced expedition to Florida with my mother so that her aging father could educate me about how Obama was a communist (on this point, O'Grady would have been in agreement). For months, I watched as a nation, terrorized, produced forms of resistance that were at once extraordinary and almost aggravatingly peaceful—like the daily anti-coup marches that were repressed with batons, chains, and such creatively vile machinery as water cannons loaded with a pepper spray solution. In October 2009, I attended the burial of Jairo Sánchez, a union leader who had been shot in the face by police. In November, I finagled a rare interview with Honduran coup general Romeo Vásquez, who kissed me on the cheek and informed me that, while he already had one wife, he would not mind having two. Vásquez was an alumnus of the United States-run School of the Americas, which had initially been located in Panama before being transferred to Fort Benning, Georgia, and where many a Latin American dictator and death squad leader had learned the tricks of the trade. He assured me that the Honduran army was composed of "very democratic soldiers."

Armed as I was with my U.S. passport, I was obviously able to extricate myself from the "long Honduran night" as needed—although I did have some long nights after awaking in the middle of one to find that a man had entered my room through the window. He quickly disappeared in the face of my banshee-like screams, but the encounter scared the shit out of me and disrupted my sleep patterns for the next decade or so. For most of my time in Tegucigalpa, I stayed in a five-dollar-per-night room in the Hotel Nan King on Avenida Gutemberg, which was run by a family that had immigrated decades before from China and where security features included a baseball bat wielded by the family's no-nonsense patriarch, who used it to shoo away potential delinquents.

Some nights, I stayed across town at a far less charmingly crappy hotel with Arturo Cano of *La Jornada,* who had temporarily installed himself there and with whom I conducted a brief coup-fueled romance. I had met him through another Mexican journalist who had touched down in post-coup Tegucigalpa and with whom I had conducted an even briefer romance that also would never have happened under less chaotically bizarre circumstances. I do not recall the name of Arturo's hotel, though I do recall the disconcerting room number: 316, as in Battalion. After Honduras, Arturo and I maintained a sometimes-friendship interspersed with spats over important topics like my insistence on wearing my sunglasses on my head at all times, and it was for this reason that I was not speaking to him when, almost exactly twelve years after the coup in Honduras, he succeeded in springing me from Siglo XXI.

Four months after my stint in prison, meanwhile, the U.S.S. Honduras would drift slightly off course with the election in November 2021 of Zelaya's wife Xiomara

Castro, who among other things had campaigned against charter cities—or "zones of employment and economic development" (ZEDEs in the Spanish acronym), as they are locally known. The website of the Charter Cities Institute lamented that "the future of charter cities in Honduras looks dim," but brought up "several reasons the situation might not be so dire," including legal protections accorded the ZEDEs: "The U.S. - Central American Free Trade Agreement (CAFTA-DR) and the U.S. - Honduras Bilateral Investment Treaty protects projects that have American investors." In the event the ZEDE concessions were repealed, Honduras could be sued. After all, how dare the original "banana republic" dream of a "future in which Honduras is sovereign and independent of U.S. domination," to borrow Frank's words?

Sure enough, in April 2022, the Honduran Congress voted to reverse the ZEDE law—and, sure enough, American ZEDE investors plowed ahead with their investment plans. The Honduran night may now be looking less dim, but sovereignty is easier said than done, and the effects of state terror don't reverse themselves overnight. Nor does U.S. hypocrisy, which was only bumped up to another level with the April 2022 extradition of former U.S. buddy Hernández to New

York to face drug trafficking charges. Decades of neoliberal violence will continue to drive migration patterns, and there will be no shortage of Hondurans like the human rights student locked up in Siglo XXI—where the nights are also long but, with the lights never turned off, definitely not dark.

6: LINES AND LISTS

In the abridged form of life that goes on within the walls of Tapachula's legendary migrant accommodations, waiting is the primary activity. There is the seemingly interminable wait for release, whether it be via the asylum track or the deportation one. It is not so much the anticipation of the moment of discharge itself that constitutes psychological torture, but the absence of any timeframe or fixed future point at which a definitive answer—however unwanted it may be—will at least be given and the individual can begin to process their impending destiny. The anguish of not knowing recalls, to some extent, the mental predicament of family members of countless thousands of disappeared persons from El Salvador to Argentina (many, predictably, the victims of United States-sponsored dirty wars), who are thwarted from grieving or attaining any sort of emotional closure—and thereby going on with their own lives—without solid news to process regarding the fates of their loved ones. In Siglo XXI, too, lives are indefinitely suspended.

There is also the waiting-within-waiting in the prison: in the lines for pretty much everything, including to sign the never-ending rotation of lists. Pandemic be damned, the lines for telephone, toiletries, and luggage are summoned at exactly the same time, which results in a confused melee in the staging area in front of the entrance and you have to ask the person against whose ass your crotch is jammed if this is the line for phone calls: "No, it's for luggage." Inmates are disentangled from the mass a few at a time and herded into the hallway, where they are diverted into either the luggage room or a new line against the wall for the phone, while toiletries are dispensed from behind the same vertigo-inducing screen as the meals and lists.

I participated in the list, meal, and luggage lines, but my sole phone call took place during an independent outing into the hallway in the company of Migra 6, who had turned up on the morning of July 12. I had spent the night on Daniely's mattress, clutching my passport and alternately torturing myself with memories of jogging barefoot on the beach in Zipolite and trying to remember Texas geography so as to plot the most practical route for illicit return to Mexico in the event of my deportation. Where is one deported to, I wondered, if one has not resided in the U.S. for nearly twenty years? Perhaps I could request to be deported to New York, where I had gone to college and where there were people I might as well see if I was forced to be in the country. (No, I decided, because what would I even wear in New York?) Or I could fly from the United States to Turkey to Cuba prior to sorting my smuggling back into Mexico—but that would not resolve the matter of the heap of cash and other survival equipment that I had left in my house in Zipolite, where I had also prudently left the windows open in order to ensure easy access for anyone wishing to take a look around.

In short, there were a lot of known unknowns—to deploy the lingo of the recently-deceased ex-U.S. secretary of defense and ravager of Iraq Donald Rumsfeld—and I was powerless to do anything about anything. Fully aware that a lack of sleep would only exacerbate my inability to confront reality rationally, I squeezed my eyes shut, but intermittent coughing fits from a nearby mattress threw a wrench in that plan. Nor, obviously, was my claustrophobia assuaged by wearing a face mask with a blanket over my head. As detainees shifted and mumbled in their sleep and nighttime conversations from other sections of the compound wafted over, I diversified my preoccupations to things like: what if a tsunami hit Zipolite and swept away all of my money and the new computer I had bought in preparation for the day when I would become that person who did not have 52,000 Word files and photos saved to their desktop? (In my defense, there had been a tsunami warning in June of the previous year when a 7.4 magnitude earthquake had rocked Oaxaca, and I had been characteristically calm and composed throughout it all.)

I began to hyperventilate beneath my mask. The thought of having a panic attack in the confines of Siglo XXI made me panic even more, and I envisioned myself asking uniformed Inami officials when I would be removed from my straitjacket only to be told "*más tarde*." I fretted about what the other detainees—who had real existential problems—would think if they knew I was worrying about tsunamis. Mercifully, I managed to avert catastrophe and wrest hold of my mind by focusing on the calming presence of two Cuban feet in my face. I eventually attained unconsciousness and dreamed some dream that I meant to remember but forgot, awaking at an undetermined hour of morning in the land of no timekeeping devices to find Daniely sitting cross-legged on the mattress vigorously adjusting her hair and inciting the others in the vicinity to get moving, because soon they would open the door to the prison yard and it would be first come, first served for the fallen mangoes.

With a teasing glare, Daniely greeted my face mask and me: "Will you take that thing *off* you're making me sweat," and added with a snicker: "If there was COVID here we'd all be dead already." She did have a point; as Inami had made no effort to mask the prison population and since everyone was on top of each other at all times anyway, there was no sense in agonizing over coronavirus unless you wanted to drive yourself mad. I myself was not even accustomed to wearing face masks, having spent the bulk of the pandemic in the corona-bubble of Zipolite, where a half-assed experiment in masking had accompanied the erection of checkpoints on either side of the village to restrict access to area residents. The arrangement had lasted for approximately three months, from March until June of 2020, during which time mask protocol was explained to me as follows by a policeman on checkpoint duty: Just put it on before you get to the checkpoint, and then ten meters later you can take it off.

I had learned from monitoring the real world on Facebook, however, that masks were important, and whenever I emerged from the Zipolite bubble into civilization I became overzealously attached to mine, lest anyone think I was a bad person. I did remove it temporarily on that Siglo XXI morning—to a dramatic sigh of relief from Daniely—when my guilt at the prospect of having my KN95 perceived as a racist and self-righteous accessory overrode my guilt at social irresponsibility and my desire to not contract COVID. Migra 6 would later assure me, after overseeing my phone call, that the prison was virus-free and that all inmates had undergone a thorough health inspection certifying that they were in tip-top shape: "Do you think we [the *migra*] would put ourselves at risk?" From my position as an inmate who had herself received no health inspection whatsoever—and who had also caught a glimpse of the list for medical visits, which included an inmate named Belkis who reported "*malestar total*," or total malaise— this was less than persuasive reasoning.

During my check-in at Siglo XXI on July 11, Migra 4 had guaranteed that the obligatory welcome phone call to the person of my choice would take place that evening, but "*más tarde.*" It did not, and my goal the next morning was thus to badger anyone wearing a uniform until it did. First, though, I needed water, and made my way to the main room to find a single empty *garrafón*, or twenty-liter bottle. There were no guards to be seen, so, stepping over mattresses and women, I approached the prison door and knocked on it. A policewoman looked in and communicated that the person in charge of replacing the *garrafón* had not yet arrived. A brief discussion ensued about the necessity of water for survival, and it was decided that I could perform *garrafón* replacement duties, which entailed being liberated into the hallway just long enough to hoist the new bottle onto my hip and carry it back through the door. Energized by my success, I moved on to the next order of business—the phone call—but was told that the woman who handled phone calls had not yet arrived and that, in this case, there was no DIY remedy. The pileup in front of the door to the prison yard had now begun in earnest, and I headed back to my appointed chamber to utilize the toilet facilities—an experience that was rendered less unpleasant when a Salvadoran girl gifted me her remaining Inami-issued toilet paper, which I had yet to receive.

In his book *The Dispossessed: A Story of Asylum at the US-Mexican Border and Beyond*, American author and journalist John Washington has an anecdote concerning the toilets at Siglo XXI. He prefaces it: "I've been told stories of Siglo XXI. Some of them, I assume, are wildly exaggerated, but the fervor with which the exaggerations are issued, it seems, must hit at some kernel of hard truth: that Siglo XXI is an awful place to be." In this particular story, the director of a humanitarian program in Honduras, who had himself been imprisoned at the facility ten years earlier during an attempt to flee north, tells Washington that there were no toilets whatsoever, and that inmates had to go "in the corner, on the walls, on the floor."

Having confirmed from other detainees—including the protagonist of his book, a twenty-four-year-old Salvadoran asylum seeker named Arnovis who spent five nights in Siglo XXI in 2017—that there were in fact toilets, Washington speculates with regard to the man's exaggerations: "Was he trying to convey something that can't be understood unless you live it or caricature it? No home, no ground to push off from, no roof to shelter under, no toilet to flush your waste. What but unflushable, unburiable feces could more poignantly express the feeling of homelessness, statelessness?"

As I discovered, though there were toilets, there were no doors on the stalls, leaving users entirely exposed to passersby. For migrants already feeling homeless, the bathroom setup was one more manifestation of the denial of autonomy to people who, in daring to violate the sacred borders of nation-states, were forced relinquish control over the boundaries of privacy. Migra 6 would later swear to me that the doorless design was for our own *seguridad*—especially in the men's section of the prison where, she said, inmates had been known to fashion weapons from door parts and even toothbrushes.

Arnovis tells Washington about having to shit in front of dozens of people and about how, before he was locked into the main prison barrack, he was given a heads-up by one of the guards re: "who the narcos were, who to look out for." A single father from remote Corral de Mulas, in the Salvadoran department of Usulután, Arnovis had detected no other option but to flee his home in the direction of the United States after receiving death threats from the Barrio 18 gang and undergoing attempted recruitment by the rival Mara Salvatrucha (MS-13)—both of which entities, it bears mentioning, owe their origins and overpowering presence in El Salvador to United States policy.

Countless Salvadorans fled to the U.S. during the country's civil war of 1980-92, which killed more than seventy-five thousand people—with the vast majority of wartime atrocities perpetrated by a right-wing military-paramilitary-death-squad amalgamation that was obsessively funded by the U.S. and defended by Reagan administration officials, who tripped over themselves to certify that the Salvadoran government was making human rights progress even as children were being massacred. Primarily around Los Angeles, gangs formed as a means of self-defense for Salvadoran communities, and that was that—until, following the end of the civil war, the U.S. had the fine idea to deport a whole bunch of prison-hardened gang members back to a country it had just helped to destroy.

The landscape of destruction proved to be fertile terrain for a neoliberal offensive, which conveniently ensured that the formidable socioeconomic inequality that had started the war in the first place would proceed apace, thereby also facilitating gang recruitment. This in turn led to policing solutions that, like in Honduras, has entailed stuff like security forces extrajudicially executing folks for having tattoos or being otherwise suspected of gang membership. Naturally, U.S. support has sustained this meticulous comportment as well as economic oppression in general. The near-comprehensive territorial control now exerted by the Made in USA gangs has meanwhile ensured that, for many Salvadoran youth, joining up is a damned if you do, damned if you don't situation—and, with invisible boundaries delineating the respective dominions of hostile factions, an act as banal as crossing the street can be lethal. Before they even get to the international borders, then, Salvadorans must contend with innumerable internal ones.

In a 2020 paper titled "Transnational moral panic: neoliberalism and the spectre of MS-13," California State University's Dr. Steven Osuna writes that the violence conducted by marginalized groups will "never equal the viciousness of what neoliberalism and transnational capital have produced for the majority of the country—alienation, domestic uncertainty and desperation"—which have again only reinforced the draw of gangs. Noting that El Salvador entered the twenty-first century with even higher rates of poverty, inequality, and migration than at the termination of the war in 1992, Osuna shows that the "violence of poverty. . . is rooted in past and present capitalist relations of exploitation, all of which are exacerbated by neoliberalism and punitive populism." In keeping with the negligible value assigned to human life in El Salvador—literally "The Savior"—the country regularly appears on the global list of homicide capitals, as does its neighbor to the northeast. But at least Honduras ("The Depths") has a less misleading name.

This, then, was the milieu Arnovis was fleeing in 2017—four years before things got even more fun when the self-proclaimed "world's coolest dictator" Nayib Bukele, also known as the President of the Republic of El Salvador, decided to convert the country into Bitcoin Wonderland. After his five-night stay in Siglo XXI, Arnovis became one of almost one hundred thousand Central Americans who that year were

packed onto buses in Mexico and "shipped south," as
Washington writes: "They were sent back to the places
they had just fled. The world, for some of them, had
become uninhabitable."

And yet, since human survival instincts are predicated on the goal of, well, surviving, many would
flee once again—including Arnovis, whose subsequent attempt sees him kidnapped and nearly killed.
He eventually makes it to the United States border in
the company of his young daughter Meybelín—and is
then deported to El Salvador without her. Washington
transcribes Arnovis' recollection of his pre-deportation
interactions with U.S. officialdom: "They took me
to another detention center, and I asked, Where's my
daughter? And they told me, I didn't you know had a
daughter. Meybelín, I told them. Who's Meybelín? She's
my daughter."

As if the United States had not already played a
significant enough role in terrorizing El Salvador into
uninhabitability, Arnovis then has to undergo the terror of having his child not only forcibly separated from
him but officially forgotten. Thanks in part to unusually
intense media coverage of the case, the U.S. at long last
remembers who and where Meybelín is and deports her,
as well—the world uninhabitable as ever. Washington

specifies that, as per the U.S. government rulebook, "you are eligible for asylum only if you have suffered persecution *on account of an immutable characteristic*—your race, religion, nationality, political opinion, or your membership in a particular social group—and the government in your country of origin is either unwilling or unable to protect you." But what if imperial persecution is the immutable characteristic?

In the course of gathering material for *The Dispossessed*, Washington pays numerous visits to Corral de Mulas, where he is received with excessive hospitality by Arnovis' humble family, who overfeed him and make him take over Arnovis' dad's hammock—the exact opposite kind of welcome extended to Arnovis in the U.S. Change a few details, and it's the same scene I have lived over and over again from Tunisia to Tajikistan— all of which simply goes to underscore that the U.S. is on the losing end of humanity.

In *Empire of Borders*, Todd Miller recounts episodes of generosity from strangers that, for those of us who have had the privilege to roam the world, are commonplace. Commenting that "often when I travel abroad I realize that I have a lot to learn when it comes to hospitality," he introduces us to Mohammed, a Syrian refugee in Jordan who hosts Miller and colleague Gabriel Schivone:

After we took off our shoes and sat on the cushions on the floor, Mohammed told me that we were welcome in his house.

He paused, then added that we were not only welcome now, but would always be welcome in his house for the rest of our lives.

For the next few hours he brought Schivone and me coffee, cakes, tea, and cold drinks. He invited us to dinner. He invited us to stay at his house. He invited us to stay a week if we wanted.

Miller goes on to reflect that Mohammed's hospitality "felt not only refreshing but also almost subversive," especially after he and Schivone had just spent "entire days dissecting the decidedly inhospitable border enforcement situation in Jordan," where the United States was pumping $300 million into the Jordan Border Security Project and the U.S.-based Raytheon Corporation had supplied a "287-mile enforcement system" involving cameras, radars, quick reaction team vehicles, and other lucrative palliatives for U.S.-fueled quagmires in neighboring Iraq and Syria.

Anyway, I had lots to think about in the Siglo XXI bathroom stall on the morning of July 12, as I went about avoiding sitting on the toilet seat and offered my most nonchalant smile—from beneath the now guiltily replaced face mask—to the woman occupying the stall to my left. I never learned anything about the girl who had donated her remaining toilet paper to me, beyond the fact that she was Salvadoran and a true savior.

I had spent three months in San Salvador just prior to the pandemic and, had I not urgently needed to attend to menstrual issues, could certainly have struck up a conversation with the girl based on that commonality. However, keen though I was to know everyone's story, I was also wary of using my fellow inmates as my own personal captive population for journalistic exploitation. People who were already physically and emotionally exposed on every level did not need some gringa running around interrogating them about their tragedies to boot.

As a privileged outsider, El Salvador had for me been entirely habitable, exempt as I was from the ubiquitous unseen borders demarcating the domains of rival entities—and from being forcibly identified by the gang affiliation of my neighborhood of residence and having my movements circumscribed accordingly. So it was that I had spent three more-or-less blissful months drinking giant Pilsener beers and posing for photos in front of MS-13 graffiti on the beach, in between writing articles about demented U.S. antics in the region and the world and keeping tabs on a Facebook group for expats in El Salvador, whose members were forever consumed with helping each other find rental properties, robotic vacuum cleaners, Thanksgiving dinners, and Kraft Jet-Puffed Marshmallow Creme Spread. I had rented an apartment with a pleasant view of the San Salvador volcano, palm trees, and the rooftop acrobatics of an energetic squirrel on Calle Soldado Matías Alvarado, named for an allegedly fallen hero of the 1969 "Soccer War" between El Salvador and Honduras, who, it turned out, had not died at all and had even participated in the Salvadoran victory march.

According to the *SextaDécima* blogger who interviewed Alvarado's family members, the soldier had hailed, like Arnovis, from the department of Usulután, and had been assigned to the northern theater of operations during the conflict, also known as the 100 Hour War. There, he had reportedly enjoyed the command of none other than José "Chele" Medrano: director of the Salvadoran National Guard, CIA liaison, and founder of, inter alia, the U.S.-backed rural paramilitary network ORDEN that—as the *New York Times* put it— "operated as a death squad that killed peasants who tilted to the left."

Uruguayan writer Eduardo Galeano once described the Soccer War as pitting against each other two "dictatorships forged at a U.S. factory called the School of the Americas." For some reason, Alvarado was marked down as a war casualty, although his wife did not find out about his death, as he arrived home quicker than the news did—despite being nearly martyred en route to his house, when a friend from the village invited him to drinks and proceeded to deliver a machete blow to his back. Alvarado never fully recovered from the incident, but he eventually found a job with the National Administration of Aqueducts and Sewers, and died in 1995, twenty-six years after his original death, at his home in the San Salvador suburb of Soyapango—today one of the most notoriously gang-saturated areas of the capital.

It's anyone's guess as to how Alvarado was not only erroneously reported dead but also deemed deserving of his very own street. In any case, the difference between life and death in El Salvador is often slim.

7: THE WAITING GAME

You have to calm down, Migra 6 ordered me. Otherwise, you'll get sick and we'll have to keep you here longer.

This, obviously, was the most calming of all possible threats—and was delivered while Migra 6 was still holding the phone receiver through which I had just blubberingly spoken to my mother in the U.S. A mere four days earlier, she and my father had celebrated the birth of their first grandchild, my younger brother's son, and I apparently could not let them relish the moment without reminding them that their own firstborn was also succeeding impressively at life.

For the placement of my "arrival" phone call, which took place sixteen-ish hours after it was supposed to, I stood in the hallway in front of the main reception area where Migra 4 had supervised my dispossession. Migra 6 stood across a counter from me, in the office that occupied half of the space in the luggage room and, after dialing my mom's number and passing me the phone, kept half an eye on me while partaking of some snacks and gossip with Migras 7 through 10 or 11. In addition to tasking my mother with figuring out how to get me out of there, I asked her to email my editor at Al

Jazeera to notify her that I would not be submitting my next article on time.

Being wiser than I, my parents immediately thought to contact Arturo Cano, the *La Jornada* journalist, after the U.S. embassy in Mexico City had fed them the line about not interfering in Mexican affairs. With my editor's help, they tracked him down, and, judging from what Arturo told me later, my mother maintained a façade of composure on the phone while my dad went about totally losing it in the background. When, upon my release, I found out that it had been Arturo who had gotten me out—by contacting AMLO's spokesperson as well as a political friend who then contacted the director of Inami—I was initially peeved that I was forcibly indebted to him after our latest spat about me wearing my sunglasses on my head. I quickly reasoned, however, that it was preferable to owe my freedom to Arturo Cano than to the U.S. government.

The phone call had at long last come about when Migra 6 had grown tired of me stalking her. I had completed my matutinal bathroom experience just in time to witness the grand unlocking of the door to the prison yard and the eruption of incarcerated bodies into fresher-but-still-incarcerated air; Daniely had secured herself a spot near the front, where, hands placed on the shoulders of the woman in front of her, she had been prancing in place like an athlete on the sidelines. Migra 5, a new face, had overseen the opening of the door, which was met with a collective whooping cry and forward charge as the room emptied.

I drifted outside, where the sun felt abnormally hostile and disorienting. A Haitian woman lay facedown on the cement, which seemed as good a summary of the situation as any. I was in the midst of debating whether it would be feasible to jog around the sports court in shoes with no laces—and thereby work at expelling the jinn that was known to take up residence in my being whenever I was too idle—when I was intercepted by an eighteen-year-old Honduran named María, who asked where I was from and accordingly howled with laugher when I told her.

María was trying to reach the United States for an operation on her hands, she told me, because Honduras was fucked and the president was a narco. Actually, she continued, I was not the only unusual admission to Siglo XXI; there had also been an older Canadian woman with a habit of relieving herself in locations that were not the toilet and repeating—in broken Spanish and at top volume—that she did not want to be there. María and some of the other detainees had tried to comfort the woman, she said, but the logistics were complicated, and anyway she had been released after a couple of days. My country would surely rescue me, too, María wagered, and I'd be out in no time.

I next set about pestering two policewomen strolling across the grass, who pointed across the prison yard at the newly materialized Migra 6, the ticket to my phone call. I made haste to present myself, and steeled my emotions against a descent into a Stockholm Syndrome scenario when she addressed me as "*mi amor.*" She also introduced a new element to the mix: the *jurídico*, with whom I supposedly had to meet and who was integral to my freedom. I never did find out exactly who or what the *jurídico* was, only that he was supposed to arrive at nine o'clock, then ten or eleven, then sometime in the afternoon or maybe the next day.

I devoted myself to hovering conspicuously in the vicinity as Migra 6 made rounds of the inmates, which eventually paid off when she announced: "*Vamos, mi amor.*" There followed the phone call, the mid-phone call mini-breakdown, the post-phone call maxi-breakdown and the helpful threat about not getting sick. As I had yet to speak with the *jurídico*, I was not even really in the pipeline and, according to Migra 6, the paperwork that would have to be sorted out in conjunction with the U.S. embassy to secure my release was liable to drag out indefinitely. In the event that I was not able to pull myself together, Migra 6 declared as I sobbed into my face mask, I could add my name to the list to see the prison psychologist—which at least momentarily distracted me from my breakdown as I pondered what sort of person the Siglo XXI psychologist might be.

Then it was back into the holding pen—"patience, *mi amor*"—for more waiting interspersed with inquiries re: the ETA of the elusive *jurídico*. At some point shortly after I had snagged the Bic pen and it had ceased to function, my name was called. A woman with a long ponytail appeared in front of me—Migra 12 or so, I had lost count—and proclaimed, with evident amazement at the coincidence, that she was somehow related to my mother. This was not at all the case, of course, as my mother's relations are almost exclusively racists from Florida, but I played along in the interest of seeing what I could get out of this sudden kinship. "What are you *doing* in here?" Migra 12 exclaimed, finding it difficult to conceal her amusement. I rolled my eyes and dissembled about my visa not being in the system. She pledged to do her best to find out what was up with the *jurídico* and to have the Bic pen replaced, which it was not.

As I would later discover, Migra 12 was in fact a relative of the husband of a Japanese-American friend of my Polish former hitchhiking companion Amelia, who had herself married a Mexican man and was now living in Mérida on the Yucatán peninsula. My parents evidently had contacted not only Arturo but also everyone else they could think of around the world, including my intermittent boyfriend in Lebanon, who had then contacted Amelia's husband, who had contacted the husband of the Japanese-American and relative of Migra 12. This man, whose name was Roberto, had himself traveled undocumented to the United States, where "not being in the system" naturally entailed far more comprehensive torment and where he and his wife had jumped through all manner of costly hoops in an effort to convince the U.S. government that he was worthy of being pronounced "legal."

My name was next called during lunch—my name of course being "Estados Unidos"—and this time I was summoned into the hallway. I had been sitting at a table with Daniely and the Cuban reading Dante's *Inferno*, as well as another Cuban who, seeing that I was not consuming my imitation flan, asked if she could have it. It had not been my choice to eat lunch at all, but Migra 5 had noticed that I was glumly abstaining and had pulled a similar line as Migra 6: If you don't eat, you'll get sick and we'll have to keep you here longer. As I figured it was just as likely that I would get sick from eating as from not, I had made no move—and so she personally escorted me to the vertigo-screen from behind which meals were dispensed, forcing me to cut in line. "Bread or tortillas?" asked an upbeat young man whose good humor was out of place but which I appreciated nonetheless; after all, life can't be all that much more enjoyable for the food servers and janitors of the twenty-first century than for its prisoners.

When I was summoned to the hall, my tablemates assumed I was being released, and Daniely winked at me: "See, Estados Unidos?" Two men and a woman, none of them the *jurídico* but rather more Migras, interrogated me further me about my visa situation. With her cell phone, the woman took a picture of me against the wall, and then made off with my passport to "verify the legitimacy of the document." I was sent back to lunch passport-less, which would cause yet more complications later in the day.

My next contact with Migra 6, meanwhile, took place in the luggage room, where I had come with a plot to not only collect spare underwear and clothes but also to give my face a furious tweezing—which, thanks to disproportionately hairy Spanish-Cuban ancestry, was usually necessary once every few hours—and to smuggle my pen into jail by hiding it in the change of clothes. Unfortunately, a ransacking of my bags revealed that both tweezers and pen had been seized. Nor was I permitted to utilize drawstring shorts without having Migra 6 cut the strings off ("for your *seguridad, mi amor*"); ditto for the strings on my hoodie. Migra 6 had meant to look for a book for me to read, she told me, but she had not had time. As for the *jurídico*, he hadn't turned up today, but there was always tomorrow.

Back inside, I resumed my position in front of the vertigo-screen in case anyone in uniform wandered into the office and could be harassed for updates as to the status of my detention or at least replace the pen. Then, suddenly, I was waved over by a group of Haitian women sitting at a nearby table who, confirming that I spoke English, announced with enthusiasm that they had found a "friend" for me: "Bangladesh," Siglo XXI's sole Bangladeshi detainee, slouched over and staring into oblivion at the end of the table. The Haitians explained in minimal English and hand gestures that they had tried to assist her but that the language barrier made this difficult. Maybe I could help?

Bangladesh rose from her seat and greeted me. Small-framed and apologetic—as though she were taking me away from some very important life I was otherwise leading—she said that she just wanted to find out two things: how long she would have to remain in jail, and whether she would be permitted to stay in Mexico or be deported to her home country. She spoke no Spanish and could not communicate with the jailers, so back we went to the vertigo-screen, which continued to make me dizzy via my peripheral vision even as I was conversing with Bangladesh.

It had taken her nine months to reach Tapachula from home, a journey that had involved a dizzying number of countries and would have ideally ended in the U.S. She had come with her husband, currently in the men's section of Siglo XXI which, he had reported to her, was a terribly violent environment. Here in the women's section, Bangladesh suspected, they must put sleep-inducing substances in the food, because she was normally unable to doze off in the company of strangers—much less hundreds of them packed tightly together under bright lights. Not only did she sleep all night, she said, she also slept much of the day. Indeed, I would later see her on her mattress against the wall—beneath the multilingual instructions for how to go about seeking asylum in Mexico—her blanket covering her head in an eerie evocation of Guantánamo.

Thanking me repeatedly for my time, Bangladesh then broke down in tears—for which she also apologized—while describing how the worst thing about it all was the suffering she was causing her mother back home, with whom she had managed to speak on the telephone. Her mother's anguish was taking a toll on her own mental health, she said, and she did not know how much longer she could go on in such a state. Fully aware of the absurdity of my words even as I pronounced them—"It'll be okay"—I put my hand on her shoulder, she put her hand on mine, and we stood there in a twenty-first-century Bangladesh-Estados Unidos solidarity statue until movement was detected behind the vertigo-screen and it was time to pounce.

I don't even remember at this point if the woman was a Migra or some other category of official, but whoever she was, she was unable to furnish any information other than that the answers to Bangladesh's two questions would depend on decisions made at some future juncture by people who were not her. Bangladesh nodded, a blank look having replaced the tears in her eyes, and, thanking me again, returned to sit with the Haitians, who wrote off my dismal failure with a couple of smiles and shrugs.

Haiti was well represented in Siglo XXI, as it was in the larger *ciudad-cárcel*—jail city—of Tapachula where, by certain accounts, there were more Haitians than Mexicans these days. The woman who had in my own pre-incarcerated days served me juice at the market downtown had, for example, estimated that *haitianos* now outnumbered *chiapanecos* by a ratio of five to two—useful mathematics, no doubt, from a xenophobia-mongering standpoint. Two months later, in September, the *Los Angeles Times* would more reasonably put the entire migrant population of Tapachula—alternately described as a "sweltering city," a "vast open-air detention camp," and a "polyglot choke point"—at maybe 50,000, above and beyond the town's "usual" population of about 350,000.

As many as half of the migrants, the *Times* surmised, were Haitians who had fled to Chile and Brazil in the aftermath of the January 2010 earthquake that had collapsed Haiti and who were now in "exodus" once again, spurred on by pandemic-related financial hardship. *La Jornada* would meanwhile report that the "flood" of Haitian migrants seeking to transit Mexico to the United States in 2021 was threatening to "collapse" the very operation of COMAR, the Mexican Commission for Refugee Assistance, which had as of September already received more than eighteen thousand Haitian asylum applications and more than three thousand from "'Chileans and Brazilians' who are in reality the children of Haitian refugees in those nations."

According to COMAR head Andrés Ramírez, the majority of these people would "not qualify as refugees"—as though you couldn't still be a refugee if you had already been one in Chile or Brazil, or as though there was somehow an expiration date for a general historical context of oppression. Never mind that, as per the outline of Mexico's Law on Refugees, Complementary Protection, and Political Asylum that appears on the website of the United Nations High Commissioner for Refugees (UNHCR), the qualification of "refugee" can apply to, inter alia, persons who "are outside of their country of nationality and don't have the protection of their country" or who "have fled their country because their life, security or liberties have been threatened by widespread violence, foreign aggression, internal conflicts, massive breach of human rights, or other circumstances that have severely disrupted the public order."

Objectively speaking, Haitians can claim pretty much any or all of the above, and the United States has had a considerable hand in guaranteeing these "circumstances." Even in cases of disruption of the public order that are technically out of U.S. hands, such as natural disasters, the global hegemon has managed to intensify the severity of the crisis. Shortly after the 2010 earthquake, the *New York Times* announced that "America has a message for the millions of Haitians left homeless and destitute by last week's earthquake: Do not try to come to the United States."

The article went on to explain the following judicious allocation of U.S. taxpayer resources: "Every day, a United States Air Force cargo plane specially equipped with radio transmitters flies for five hours over the devastated country, broadcasting news and a recorded message" from the Haitian ambassador in Washington, that—like Kamala Harris' 2021 memo to Guatemala: "Do not come"—sought to deter folks from extricating themselves from devastation. Thus far, the *Times* specified, United States officials had detected "no sign of Haitians trying to flee the island by boat," but were nonetheless "laying plans to scoop up any boats carrying illegal immigrants and send them to Guantánamo Bay, Cuba."

Haiti, of course, was already quite familiar with the workings of everyone's favorite illegal offshore penal colony. Haitians had been the facility's first guests in the 1990s, when thousands of Haitian refugees were

subjected to indefinite detention upon fleeing the
1991 U.S.-backed military coup against Jean-Bertrand
Aristide (not to be confused with the 2004 U.S.-backed
coup against Jean-Bertrand Aristide). Nor was this the
first instance of United States "foreign aggression. . .
or other circumstances that have severely disrupted the
public order" in Haiti. Jonathan M. Katz, former AP
correspondent in Port-au-Prince and author of *The Big
Truck That Went By: How the World Came to Save Haiti
and Left Behind a Disaster*, writes at *Foreign Policy* that "US
elites began setting their sights on Haiti" in the 1910s,
more than a century after the Haitian slave revolution
had won the territory independence from France and
pissed off powerful white people around the world. As
punishment for this barbaric crime of self-governance,
Haiti was subsequently forced to pay reparations to her
former French masters—an irreparably ludicrous business for which the United States was fully on board, as
bankrupted Haitian governments were obliged to take
out gargantuan loans from American and other banks.

Then in December of 1914, "on the pretense of
ensuring repayment of those loans (particularly those
owed to Citibank in New York), a team of U.S. Marines
came ashore in Port-au-Prince, charged into the central
bank of Haiti, and took half the nation's gold reserves

to a vault on Wall Street," as one does. National drama predictably ensued, including the killing of short-lived Haitian president Vilbrun Guillaume Sam, whereupon Woodrow Wilson "used the assassination his policies had helped foment as the pretext for an all-out invasion" of Haiti, resulting in a U.S. occupation that lasted nearly two decades and was characterized by a "mixture of paternalism and brutality." This worked well economically for the United States, and was rendered more efficient when U.S. Marines "replaced Haiti's army with a client militarized police force and reimposed forced, unpaid labor, performed at gunpoint, to build a road system to ensure military and commercial control." Sounds kind of like slavery.

Moving along to the 1950s, Harsha Walia details in *Border and Rule: Global Migration, Capitalism, and the Rise of Racist Nationalism* how the United States continued to keep Haiti in alignment with its ever-imperative "interests." These were served by the likes of despots François "Papa Doc" Duvalier and his offspring Jean-Claude "Baby Doc" Duvalier, who "killed tens of thousands of Haitians, imprisoned even more in the dreaded Fort Dimanche torture camp, and fueled a massive exodus of refugees, yet were propped up by the US for nearly three decades as counterpoints to communist Cuba."

More recent U.S. administrations, too, have forcefully defended capitalist interests in Haiti, as when the Obama administration—specifically the State Department commanded by Hillary Clinton as well as USAID—conspired to block an increase in the minimum wage beyond 31 cents per hour for Haitian assembly-zone workers toiling on behalf of U.S. clothing manufacturers. Anyway, U.S. corporations need to eat, too.

Meanwhile, the United States has never been one to let a "massive exodus" go to waste and, as Walia documents, the "interdiction and detention of Haitian refugees during the 1980s and 1990s laid the groundwork for the US onshore and offshore immigration detention system in place today." Although the maritime border between the U.S. and the Caribbean is not in the spotlight as much as the U.S.-Mexico frontier, she emphasizes, the United States' historically sadistic handling of Haitians in Guantánamo and elsewhere "preceded most onshore policies of mass detention and illustrates the multiplication of US bordering practices across spaces."

To be sure, you could not have asked for a better encapsulation of imperial fuckery—and the unilateral U.S. right to wantonly violate other people's borders—than taking a mass of people fleeing the United States' devastation of one country and imprisoning them in a military base on illegally occupied territory in a different one, Cuba, with which the United States at the time had no diplomatic relations. As for current outsourced U.S. bordering practices across the space of southern Mexico, Haitians and Cubans were pretty much in the same boat in 2021—and not just in Tapachula. Further to the south, the Voice of America website reported in August, these two nationalities were the "most prevalent" at the Darién Gap, the deadly stretch of jungle between Colombia and Panama, where the Cubans of Siglo XXI had told me of all the people who had gone in one end and never emerged and the thirteen-year-old girl who had been repeatedly raped along the way.

VOA quoted Raúl López, a projector coordinator in Panama for Médecins Sans Frontières/Doctors Without Borders, on how migrants "get robbed" with great frequency in the Darién, "and if they are traveling with women, most of them — they get raped." Indeed, it should be vicariously traumatizing to anyone with half a soul that such violations of human bodies effectively occur as a direct result of the selective inviolability of the U.S. border—while everyone else's borders remain up for the violating. According to statistics from the United Nations Children's Agency (UNICEF) cited by VOA, of the more than four thousand children that had crossed the Darién Gap in the first six months of 2021, half had been younger than five. Between January and April, more than two hundred pregnant women crossed, most of them in their third trimester.

In response to VOA's "query about any U.S. role in the Darién Gap," a State Department spokesperson had emailed some lines about working with the Panamanian government to "improve Panama's national asylum capacity; ability to address irregular migration; ability to provide protection and basic humanitarian aid to asylum seekers, refugees, and vulnerable migrants; and promote safe, orderly, and humane alternatives to continuing a journey northward." This was a far more straightforward and practical solution than, say, not messing up other people's countries in the first place. And yet it has never been the point of U.S. capitalism to actually resolve things, but rather to find lucrative nonsolutions to the problems it causes.

The VOA dispatch also mentioned another voice of America, as it were: Homeland Security secretary Alejandro Mayorkas, who on July 13—one day after my release from Siglo XXI, incidentally—had echoed the refrain of so many previous American voices. "Allow me to be clear," he said in an announcement directed specifically at the inhabitants of Haiti and Cuba. "If you

take to the sea, you will not come to the United States."
Over the course of imperial U.S. history, there has been
a rich supply of can't-make-this-shit-up moments, and
this was definitely one of them: Mayorkas himself had
come to the United States as a baby from none other
than Cuba, his family having fled the island in 1960,
the year after the triumph of the Cuban Revolution had
crushed the U.S.-backed dictatorship in favor of a more
equal society and other annoying stuff.

As luck would have it, members of my own family
had gotten to revel in the legendary excesses of Cuba
during its prerevolutionary incarnation as international
elite playground—like my great-uncle Benito, born in
the Ybor City neighborhood of Tampa, Florida, to a
Cuban mother named Belén from the village of Campo
Florido outside Havana. This original Belén, who
entered the world in 1894 and moved to the U.S. with
her sister around 1905, was a humble woman who never
acquired much English beyond an approximation of the
names for a select number of fruits, but she did know
the words to 359 Spanish songs by heart, as tallied by
one of her daughters during a long car trip in the 1960s.
In her Ybor City backyard, she had a cow, chickens,
and, once, an illegally kept pig, who had to be hidden
from inspectors.

Benito ended up back in Cuba in the 1950s, summoned by his childhood friend from Ybor City, mafia boss Santo Trafficante Jr.—the son of mafia boss Santo Trafficante Sr. In Havana, Benito was assigned surveillance duties at the Sans Souci nightclub and casino belonging to the younger Trafficante, a close friend of dictator Fulgencio Batista, while also performing other underworldly functions. As per a June 1959 memorandum from "Legal Attaché, Havana" to FBI director J. Edgar Hoover, a certain "HAV-33" had recently "advised that BENITO FERNANDEZ continued to be the Manager of the Hotel Comodoro gambling casino for SANTO TRAFFICANTE."

When the Cuban playground closed, Benito reintegrated himself into the racket of mainstream capitalism and sold furniture in a Miami shopping mall. Mayorkas, for his part, went about accumulating lessons from his own family's trajectory that would later serve him professionally. "Through his Cuban-born father," *The Washington Post* reminisces, "he learned someone can love a country and still feel compelled to leave it forever." And through his Romanian-born mom, "whose relatives were murdered by the Nazis, Mayorkas discovered the horrors that can unfold when refugees cannot flee to safety."

Mayorkas' July 13 Haitian- and Cuban-specific warning had been triggered not only by an uptick in U.S.-bound migration by both nationalities that year but also by tumultuous events in each country over the preceding days. In Cuba, the July 11 protests over widespread scarcities had propelled the pathologically vindictive Cuban exile gang into fits of ecstasy at the prospect of the United States charging in to save Cuba from the situation in which it had put Cuba. And in Haiti, the assassination of President Jovenel Moïse on July 7—the very day of my arrival to Tapachula from Zipolite— produced similar, shall we say, wargasms. In his *Foreign Policy* intervention, titled "U.S. Intervention in Haiti Would Be a Disaster—Again," Katz remarks that "the blood had barely dried on the floor of. . . Moïse's bedroom before calls for U.S. involvement began"—and to hell with the fact that "poverty and chaos" in Haiti had been "shaped by Washington for decades."

Katz makes clear that, just as Woodrow Wilson's Marines did not have to directly orchestrate the assassination of a Haitian president in order to achieve the pretext for invasion and occupation of the country, "no part of the U.S. government had to be directly involved in Moïse's assassination for Haiti's current crisis to be born out of U.S. domination in 2021." Despite

including Haiti on his 2018 list of "shithole countries"—
along with El Salvador and assorted African nations—
Donald Trump "enabled [Moïse's] dictatorial tendencies
through continued affirmative support," as did the ensuing Biden administration, while Moïse and his accom-
plices "unleashed terror, allowing violent gangs, police,
and elements of the remobilized Haitian army to carry
out vicious massacres aimed at intimidating the population into submission." This is to name but a few of the,
um, "horrors that can unfold when refugees cannot flee
to safety."

The year of the United States assault on the central
bank of Haiti that set the stage for all manner of horrors,
1914 had been busy for Wilson's Marines—including
in Mexico. The website of the Woodrow Wilson
Presidential Library and Museum in Staunton, Virginia
features a section on that year's "Incident at Tampico,"
the Mexican port city in the state of Tamaulipas where
"American warships were sitting just off the coast to
protect American oil interests." A 1913 coup against
Mexican President Francisco I. Madero had resulted in
the ascension to power of General Victoriano Huerta,
the opposition to whom the new U.S. ambassador to
Mexico had set about backing with "loans and support,
while keeping the door open for military interventions."

This after the previous U.S. ambassador "had been involved in the plot to overthrow Madera [*sic*] that brought Huerta to power."

So the warships were just hanging out at sea when, all of a sudden, nine U.S. sailors were detained by Huerta's forces. The Woodrow Wilson website continues: "The commander of US forces in the area demanded a 21-gun salute and an apology from Huerta after the sailors were quickly released. When the Mexican government refused, the situation became tense, and President Wilson used the events as a reason to request permission from Congress for an armed invasion of Mexico. Events soon led to the occupation of Veracruz by US forces." On its timeline of U.S.-Mexico relations, the website of the Council on Foreign Relations offers a slightly different version of the Tampico Affair, in which the nine sailors are arrested for having allegedly entered a prohibited zone—after which "Mexico apologizes, but U.S. President Woodrow Wilson sends Marines to the port of Veracruz to 'obtain from General Huerta and his adherents the fullest recognition of the rights and dignity of the United States.'"

In other words, it has never been permissible to apply the concept of "Do not come" to the United States itself, the rights and dignity of which are insulted and trampled by other nations' pretenses to sovereignty. As for other dignified matters, the Council on Foreign Relations pinpoints "migration" as the "root of the first dispute" between the United States and Mexico— but not the sort of migration that currently entails the obliteration of the rights and dignity of persons fleeing U.S.-fueled calamity. The year on the timeline is 1830, and Mexico has opted to ban immigration to Texas from the U.S. as well as to abolish slavery. Undeterred, American settlers persist in their conquest of freedom and, after scoring independence from Mexico in 1836, Texas joins the United States as a slave state in 1845. And presto: "dispute" resolved. Having lived in Austin myself from the age of seven to seventeen and been forced to endure various years of Texas history class, I can attest that certain pertinent details—such as the fact that Texas belonged to Mexico, and that the city in which I resided was named for a colonizer and slaveowner—were downplayed in favor of emotional remembrances of the Alamo and the vilification of Mexican leader Antonio López de Santa Anna.

Fast-forward from the nineteenth to the twenty-first century, and the gringo attitude of self-righteous entitlement holds fast. Mexico, a victim of U.S. policies of xenophobia and racism, is roped into enforcing a border regime that replicates those policies. Just as images of black migrants being effectively hunted on horseback by U.S. border personnel shocked the internet of 2021, photos of Inami agents manhandling Haitians confirm that official bigotry is highly contagious. It is only fitting that the Zapatistas—who from the get-go called out the neoliberal sacking of Mexico known as NAFTA and who commenced their uprising in Chiapas on January 1, 1994, the day the agreement went into effect—would slam the AMLO administration for the "inhumane treatment" of migrants seeking to break free of Tapachula, Chiapas' number one *ciudad-cárcel* and a neoliberal landmark unto itself. But while inhumanity clearly knows no borders, might it also, in the end, be a sort of prison for those who propagate it?

8: THE (FORGOTTEN) PASSPORT TO FREEDOM

Perhaps Bangladesh was right and they really did put something somniferous in the food, I thought while I drifted in and out of sleep, though it was still the afternoon. It was raining and a dampness had pervaded all things in Siglo XXI, including my mattress and blanket. I no longer had the energy, it seemed, to feel anxious or depressed, or to attend to anything aside from the sound of the rain on the prison roof— not the shouting going on above and around me, not the Haitian sitting on my feet. Decidedly not an optimist by nature, I nonetheless began to reckon—as I let fatigue overwhelm me—that indefinite imprisonment was not a bad opportunity to catch up on all the sleep I had missed out on over the past thirty-nine years. The last time I'd had a decent slumber was in 2013 when, deprived of internet and technology for four blissful days during a camping expedition in remote Oman, I flabbergasted myself by clocking an unprecedented ten-plus hours a night under the stars, clear proof that I had up till then been going about life all wrong. The only other human my camping friends and I encountered on the trip was an Omani shepherd, who was clearly going about things right and who probably slept like this every night, I told myself.

But then it was on to nearby Dubai and everything that was wrong with life and the world—unless you happen to be a fan of heavily surveilled police states built on slave labor where basic human rights are nonexistent but you can go skiing in a mall surrounded by scorching desert. In a 2006 essay titled "Fear and Money in Dubai," historian and urban theorist Mike Davis wrote of the Emirati city-state as epitomizing "apocalyptic luxuries"—a "coastal desert" that had become a "huge circuit board upon which the elite of transnational engineering firms and retail developers are invited to plug in high-tech clusters, entertainment zones, artificial islands, glass-domed 'snow mountains,' *Truman Show* suburbs, cities within cities—whatever is big enough to be seen from space and bursting with architectural steroids."

Dubai, incidentally, had been the first stop for Bangladesh and her husband on their nine-month odyssey to Mexico—no doubt a fitting start to a trajectory that would encapsulate the apocalyptic discrepancy between transnational navigation by elite capital and transnational navigation by those whose permanent exploitative subjugation is necessary to do things like build Dubai. Freedom of speech is tightly restricted in the United Arab Emirates, and the slightest criticism of the government can land you in jail—but the federation of sheikhdoms boasts a Minister of State for Happiness and Wellbeing to ensure that it remains the happiest little police state ever.

The United States, of course, is perfectly happy with Dubai and the rest of the UAE—especially after the Emiratis royally screwed over the Palestinians by normalizing relations with Israel—and many a U.S. bomb has contributed to the Saudi-Emirati-led apocalypse in Yemen, where the UAE military has also engaged in sexual torture and helped to inflict famine. Though I would remain in Dubai only a couple of days prior to heading to Lebanon—itself perennially on the verge of apocalypse thanks in no small part to Israel's neighborly machinations—it was enough to reverse any lingering healing effects of the Oman experiment, and I resigned myself to the probability that I would never be an Omani shepherd or sleep well again.

In Siglo XXI, on the other hand, things were looking up on the shut-eye front. Without digital stimuli keeping me unnaturally alert at all hours, I could feel my mind shutting down—retreating into some pretechnological Eden, more precisely, which happened to resemble Oman, where I was free to hibernate forever or at least until I had to pee or sign another list. So intense was my stupor that, when I did manage to drag myself to the toilet, I was actually looking forward to collapsing anew on my damp mattress and ceasing, for all intents and purposes, to exist.

And yet, as luck would have it, I was mid-squat in the doorless stall when I heard my name being successively called down the corridor, culminating in Daniely's distinctly authoritative "Estados Unidos!" issued from a few meters away. I yanked up my shorts and scrambled to present myself. Migra 6 was standing in the doorway, and commanded me to "hurry up" and gather my belongings, as though we were suddenly without time. Still dazed and unconvinced that I was being released, I sought confirmation from Daniely, who was now perched atop her folded mattress inspecting her fingernails, and who looked up at me with an impish grin: "Think about us once in a while."

Eden having come to an abrupt end, I now wanted to smack myself for having agitated for my freedom if it meant just being deported to the U.S., which was itself nothing more than another variety of twenty-first-century prison. I gathered my notebook and Palestinian soap, handed off my extra Inami-issued sanitary napkins to the first bidder, and donated the still untouched *paterna-cuajinicuil-chalahuite* fruit to Daniely and another Cuban, who were initially intrigued but failed to hide their distaste once Migra 6 had instructed them on how to pry it open and ingest it.

Snapping her fingers, Migra 6 indicated for me to gather my mattress and blanket, as well, and to follow her. This, apparently, was my cue to resume being an awkward caricature, and I trotted clumsily behind her, profusely thanking everyone I passed and feeling like an utter dick for getting out of there in twenty-four hours. We rushed through the heavy metal door and into the hallway, where I deposited mattress and blanket, rushed onward to the luggage room, where I grabbed my belongings, and then rushed into the reception area, which was currently serving as a deportation staging area for a group of Hondurans—and which left me ever more certain that I, too, was being deported. Once through that door, the need to hurry terminated, and Migra 6 abandoned me for the time being to the care of two policewomen, who monitored my movements with interest ("What is that?" "A vitamin") while imposing order where necessary.

For example, when I undertook to re-lace my tennis shoes, I was warned that, were I to go ahead with the full re-lacing, I would not be allowed to put the shoes on my

feet until I had exited the prison doors—there evidently
still being a danger that I might choose to hang myself
during the process of liberation with laces firmly tied
on shoes I was wearing. There was no longer a ban on
writing utensils, however, and the nearest policewoman
even lent me her pen.

Upon learning that I was a journalist, the policewoman asked if she could come with me to the U.S.,
and if my newspaper could perhaps give her a job.
Alternatively, she said, I could hire her as a guide in
Chiapas. Unsure of what the proper answer was to such
questions when posed by an armed guard who was holding me captive, I asked her what was going on in the
indigenous municipality of Pantelhó, where a conflict
involving state security forces, paramilitaries, vigilan-
tes, narcos, and a lot of displaced humans had been one
of the last headlines I had seen pre-incarceration—and
which I figured combined the themes of journalism and
Chiapas. She shook her head and specified that her services came with a price, and that, until I was paying her,
she would divulge no information.

According to the notes I took with her pen, she
then asked me if I was from the LGBT community and
suggested that the soon-to-be-deported Honduran next
to me—who had complimented my eyes and remarked

with a warm smile that they appeared to have a *flor* in the middle—had been trying to woo me. This Honduran was in impressively good spirits, maybe because the anguish of limbo had finally come to an end—even if it meant being sent back to the circle of hell known as Honduras, where violence and hate crimes against LGBT+ persons (among other demographics) had escalated following the coup. By the ten-year anniversary of the coup in 2019, more than three hundred gay and trans people had reportedly been murdered.

As it turned out, this was not the Honduran's first visit to Siglo XXI. In fact, she had now attained professional deportee status, she declared while emitting a belly laugh and slapping the thigh of the girl sitting beside her. She could not recall how many times she'd been deported in total. When Migra 6 returned for me, she and the Honduran engaged in banter, and Migra 6 pronounced her a "good soul." It was now officially time for me to leave—although I still did not know to where. I returned the pen to the policewoman while Migra 6 saluted the Honduran: "See you next time!"

Migra 6 escorted me through the door, my laced tennis shoes in hand—an exit I then had to repeat, crossing over the threshold into the building and back out again such that Migra 6 could document the moment on her cell phone. This would be the first of many snapshots taken that afternoon, forming a proof-of-release photo series that, Arturo later told me, had been demanded of the Siglo XXI Migras by some Inami higher-up. I was photographed getting into the waiting van, and then, again, when seated in the van behind the grated partition, in the same spot I had sat the day before, with my backpack on my lap ("Smile, *mi amor*," said Migra 6, my face mask notwithstanding).

Migra 6 assumed her post in the passenger's seat. The driver's seat was occupied by Migra X, we'll call him since I had totally lost track, who greeted me with: "It's really bad in there, isn't it?" But the men's section was much worse, he and Migra 6 agreed, as it was way more overcrowded and there were mafias and fights. I thought back to Daniely's wry observation: "If this is the twenty-first century, I'd hate to see the twenty-second."

In spite of what she had assured me about rigorous health inspections for all incoming detainees, Migra 6 went on to remark under her breath to Migra X that they were in fact going about the whole COVID thing very badly in Siglo XXI. There was no time at present, however, to dwell on the implications of consciously endangering the lives of countless people who were merely seeking a chance at life, and we set off in the van in the rain for an as yet unknown destination. The mystery began to dissipate when Migra X rolled down his window to confer with another official as we pulled out onto the main road, and I overheard the word "Talismán"—this being the name of the Mexico-Guatemala border crossing just north of the one I had visited two days before in the company of Diego and Polo. We had consumed beer in plastic chairs by the Suchiate River, and had watched as rafts bearing people and products—toilet paper, detergent, more beer—floated back and forth in nonchalant defiance of the legal border regime above. Nearby, a member of the Mexican National Guard randomly harassed local pedestrians for papers, and a sign next to the river specified that both urinating and smoking were prohibited.

Upon hearing "Talismán," my brain naturally assumed that Mexico had decided to dump me in Guatemala—which was certainly better than being deported to the United States but still sort of sucked, especially as it was raining and I was almost out of cash. I couldn't bring myself to ask Migras 6 and X what the plan was, preferring instead to agonize over the possibilities, but Migra X interrupted my mental tumult with a relevant question of his own: "Where's your boyfriend?"

Without thinking, I responded "Which one?"—and then had to go on to explain how, back in the good old days when I had dashed continuously between countries like it was going out of style, it had at times proved practical to have a man in every port, as it were, albeit challenging to prevent the various parallel lives from intersecting. Migra X wanted details about some of the men: "And the one in Turkey, where does he work?"—while Migra 6 opined that it all sounded like a perfect arrangement to her.

After delving a bit into the subject of how passionate Mexican men are, Migra X got sidetracked reminiscing about his own travels, which, it so happened, had been facilitated by Inami, as he was often dispatched to accompany deportees on their journeys. So it was that he had visited El Salvador—which, he reported, had a lot of nice places despite its bad rap—and Canada, which was awesome. Migra 6 was bummed because, had she renewed her passport in time, she could have joined on the Canada trip, and taken advantage of the opportunity to see her son, who was a fitness trainer at a Canadian gym and whose picture she showed me on her phone through the grated partition. It was too bad indeed, Migra X concurred, that he, Migra 6, and Migra 6's son had not been able to hang out in Canada—just like it had been too bad when the scheduled deportation of a group of Yemenis to Turkey had been cancelled and he had missed out on the trip of a lifetime.

As we sped past the same tropical greenery that Diego, Polo, and I had sped past two days prior, Migra X shifted gears once again and asked how I would respond right now if asked to describe my Siglo XXI experience: "It was horrible? Inami treated you badly?" I said that I would say that, yes, it was horrible, but that it had also offered a glimpse of human resilience under oppression. The Migras agreed that at least I would have plenty to write about, and Migra 6 added: "Don't forget to put that you cried!" Migra X suggested that we return to discussing my boyfriends.

When we were around ten kilometers from Talismán, I decided to verify, just for the hell of it, that Migras 6 and X were in possession of my passport, whereupon they turned to look at me in synchronized horror: "You don't have your passport?" I explained that, no, the passport had been appropriated earlier in the afternoon by what I had thought was the maybe-*jurídico* but wasn't, and I had not seen it since. Migra X brought the van to a halt on the side of the road, and the Migras set about rectifying matters via their cell phones. The passport was tracked down, and someone committed to bringing it to Talismán in a separate vehicle within a certain time frame, prompting Migra X to inquire if we were talking about "real time" or other forms of time that have been known to exist in Mexico.

It was still raining when we reached the border and parked across from the immigration building in front of the bridge. Startlingly, the passport was delivered in even quicker than real time, and the brief wait was filled by Migra 6 singing along to "Wonderwall" on the van radio: "Because maybe/You're gonna be the one that saves me/And after all/You're my wonderwall."

Then it was "*Vamos, mi amor*," and into the building we went (photo time again). I was ushered into a room with an important-looking immigration officer, who welcomed me with a fist bump, told me to take a seat, and dropped a fresh *forma migratoria múltiple*—the Mexican entry permit—on the table in front of me to fill out (more photos). I don't recall the precise moment at which I realized what was going on, but it soon became obvious: Mexico was not deporting me for my transgressions but rather giving me 180 more days in the country—without even making me walk across the bridge to Guatemala and back. Arturo was efficient.

An even more important-looking immigration officer then materialized—the "*jefe de jefes*" of the border, as Migra 6 would later characterize him—who took both of my hands in his, asked if there was anything I needed, and wished me a lovely stay in Mexico. As I went over to pay for my visa at the cashier's desk, all I could think of was Daniely's smirk.

Back in the van, the Migras were in good cheer, and told me they would drop me off wherever I liked: at a friend's place, at a hotel, at the cinema. I was given the go-ahead to turn on my phone, which I did, only to draw a blank as to what to say to anyone. Finally, I texted my parents "I Am OUT," to which my mother responded with a barrage of partying face emojis, an "Arturo did it!!!!!," a "Don't ever do that again," and all the behind-the-scenes details of my liberation, including my father's proposal to bribe the Mexicans with $20,000, which the U.S. embassy had reportedly not appreciated. In the end, the Migras deposited me at the One Tapachula hotel near Diego and Polo's place, where Migra 6 finagled me the migra discount and where several more pictures were taken of me exiting the van and entering the lobby, to the bewilderment of the other guests.

In my room with a view of the Tacaná volcano, I sat on the edge of the bed and began the process of reinstating my bracelets—an undertaking that would span the course of two days—as personhood slowly seeped back into my being. A thorough review of my possessions, still bearing the bag tags with CONGO crossed out and replaced with ESTADOS UNIDOS, indicated that five items had been permanently lost to the guardians of the twenty-first century. In addition to my pen and tweezers, my yerba mate straw was gone—although there were fortunately four more waiting in Zipolite, thanks to a pandemic online buying spree that had also seen me acquire, inter alia, two fanny packs, two pairs of fuzzy pajamas in case I ever went anywhere where the temperature dropped below infernal, and no fewer than three pairs of high heels. This despite the fact that I did not usually wear shoes at all in Zipolite and could not walk in high heels in the first place. My bout of corona-capitalism, which was conducted in a half-guilty hedonistic frenzy on the website of Amazon México had, it seemed, allowed me an illusion of control over a self-destructing universe—even though, as W. E. B. Du Bois pointed out long ago, such behavior didn't really resolve anything: "Capitalism cannot reform itself; it is doomed to self-destruction. No universal selfishness can bring social good to all."

Also missing from my bags were the wax earplugs my mother had donated to me as a homicide prevention measure, for occasions when visitors to Zipolite felt the need to permeate the village with the phenomenon known as bass until seven o'clock in the morning. Lastly, the broken compact mirror that had been given to me— in unbroken state—by a Kurdish man in Istanbul in 2013 had disappeared. I had met him during the Gezi Park protests against the neoliberal authoritarian visions of Turkey's eternal leader Recep Tayyip Erdoğan, and the mirror had come in handy for inspecting the gobs of snot and mucus that had emanated from my nose and mouth during my introduction to tear gas. While the Turkish state had predictably branded the protesters alcoholic-hooligan-hoodlum-terrorists, I myself had been on the receiving end of nothing but hospitality from folks who were confronting a landscape of quite literally asphyxiating brutality. From my vantage point atop the unnaturally white sheets of the One Tapachula, it appeared that some things indeed never changed. Instead of imagining Oman that night to put myself to sleep, I imagined Daniely's feet in my face.

The next morning, I went jogging in my relaced shoes on the road in front of the hotel. Although technically also qualifying as an asphyxiating situation due to the levels of car exhaust, it was nothing short of exhilarating—particularly given that the programmed soundtrack consisted of Freddie Mercury's "Don't Stop Me Now" on repeat, courtesy of the decrepit iPod that had so attracted the attention of Migra 4. My feelings of invincibility were momentarily derailed when I ran past a gas station and viscerally recoiled at the sight of an attendant in uniform—the first of many such instances over the coming days, which would cause me to question whether they shouldn't have left me in jail for more than twenty-four hours and thereby forced me to grow some balls.

Having postponed my return to Zipolite until the following day, the next step in my post-Siglo XXI recovery was to eat a colossal hamburger, which I did in the company of Diego and Polo at a restaurant next to the Walmart where I had purchased the Manchego cheese that had ended up in the prison trash bin and the bread that I had consumed with Kimberly in the bathroom. There was a Narnia-style time warp as Diego and Polo hugged me—the sort of hugs that made captivity entirely worth it—and it seemed incomprehensible that, a mere forty-eight hours earlier, I had been binging on wine in their backyard while they endeavored to distract the cat from the bird that had fallen out of its nest. They filled me in on their last forty-eight hours' worth of efforts to assist the Haitian migrants in Tijuana—whose camp had recently been attacked—in seeking asylum in the United States, and I filled them in on the interior geography of Siglo XXI, a place whose outer layers they knew well but whose critical fortified border they had never crossed. Polo took credit for having already told me I should write a book about Atrapachula, which, he asserted, "exists because nobody is paying attention."

While still in Tapachula, I received a phone call from Mexico City. It was Sergio, the supplier of my former falsified Mexican *forma migratoria* and entry stamp, who was returning my panicked airport call of July 11 and who assured me that all of my fake paperwork was in order and that there was no problem whatsoever. His perspective remained unaltered by the news that I had just been in and out of jail, just as he had remained unfazed when I had previously alerted him to the fact that American Airlines flight 1751—on which, according to my fake *forma*, I had arrived to Mexico City from the U.S. in June—was actually a flight from Miami to San Salvador. Reiterating his availability for whatever future services I might need, Sergio wished me a pleasant afternoon.

On July 14, I flew without incident from Tapachula International to Mexico City's Benito Juárez airport—named for the source of that noble old opinion: "Among individuals as among nations, respect for the rights of others is peace"—and on to Huatulco on the coast of Oaxaca, from where it was a straight shot to Zipolite. It was Bastille Day in France and National Mac and Cheese Day in the United States, as well as being the day that Texas senator and self-appointed "fighter for liberty" Ted Cruz sounded the following alarm on Twitter: "In South Texas, we're seeing #COVID positivity rates rising and it's a direct result of illegal aliens being released into communities."

Beyond its utility as a means of pathologizing migration, of course, coronavirus was of minimal concern on its own since Americans' God-given liberty to spurn vaccines and face masks naturally trumps public health. A similarly pathological approach had aided operations on the Mexican-Guatemalan border—itself, again, merely an outsourced extension of the United States-Mexico one—prompting the Reuters report in March on the Mexican government's plan to "restrict movement on its southern border with Guatemala to help contain the spread of COVID-19" in return for vaccine goodies from the U.S. (that famous non-quid pro quo discussed by White House press secretary Jen Psaki). Given that air travel to Mexico was never restricted and that Americans, for example, had been free to come spread the disease as far and wide as they pleased, the fig leaf of responsible pandemic behavior on the Mexico-Guatemala frontier had spontaneously withered and died before it had even achieved leaf form.

In *Border and Rule*, Walia writes that the border between the United States and Mexico "must be understood not only as a racist weapon to exclude migrants and refugees, but as foundationally organized through, and hence inseparable from, imperialist expansion, Indigenous elimination, and anti–Black enslavement." The U.S. border regime, she notes, "was consolidated at the turn of the twenty-first century, within a constellation of imperial interventions, neoliberal capital flows, policies of carceral containment, and migration controls," and United States-Mexico "border rule" continues to "intersect. . . with global and domestic forms of warfare, positioned as a linchpin in the concurrent processes of expansion, elimination, and enslavement, thus solidifying the white settler power of racial exclusion and migrant expulsion." Add coronavirus to this list of preexisting plagues, and the intersection becomes an unparalleled mindfuck.

Thanks to Arturo's diplomatic dexterity and my imperial privilege, I was able to migrate from twenty-first-century carceral containment in Siglo XXI to the beach in Zipolite without having to contend with the physical U.S. border—or Ted Cruz's swarms of COVID-propagating aliens in South Texas, for that matter. And yet the border was never far away—an omnipresent constellation stretching from Bangladesh to the Darién Gap and everywhere in between.

When I arrived back to Zipolite on the evening of July 14, my landlord Horacio informed me that not much had transpired in my absence except that a crocodile had taken up residence in the mangrove next to my house—but that, not to worry, it was a mere two meters in length. The local police had helpfully roped the mangrove off with red tape, an effective border if there ever was one. I would never find out what happened to any of my fellow detainees in Tapachula, since, owing to the confiscation of my pen as well as general discombobulation, I had only a few first names to go on and no last names or contact information. Their faces, however, remain a testament to the boundless fortitude of the human spirit—and to how much better the twenty-first century should be.

9: RETURNING TO NOWHERE IN PARTICULAR

In Siglo XXI, as I imagine is the case in most prisons around the world, the walls speak. Names, numbers, and drawings are etched into the concrete—a noteworthy feat in itself, given that all objects with etching capabilities have ostensibly been confiscated at the prison entrance. Even more remarkably, some of the engravings occur at heights only reachable by ladder or human totem pole. If one finds oneself with all the time in the world to ponder the logistics, one's brain may conjure up more innovative scenarios to explain the elevated graffiti—such as levitating inmates or walls that spontaneously invert themselves, unbeknownst to the jailers.

A memorial to unquantifiable suffering, the markings are also an affirmation of existence in the face of a ruthlessly dehumanizing scheme that punishes the poor for trying to survive. I did not make my mark on the prison walls, nor did I deserve to. My twenty-four hours in Siglo XXI were just that: another day of life—if a rather atypical one—for a privileged inhabitant of earth. I had not risked my life to get there, and I would not be deported to potential death. All I had to deal with was the crocodile, which was finally captured after a few weeks and taken away.

Once back in Zipolite, I set about not settling down, and gradually resumed my pre-pandemic itinerant ways—albeit this time using the coastal village as an international base. I flew to Turkey and Albania for two months, and returned to Zipolite. I flew to Cuba for a month, and returned to Zipolite. I even flew to the U.S. for the first time in six years, my self-imposed exile having been thwarted by the birth of my first nephew as well as my parents' decision to return to the homeland from Barcelona.

At the beginning of April 2022, I was preparing to travel from Zipolite to San Salvador, after which I would hit up Lebanon, Turkey, Greece, Bulgaria, and whatever else I managed to fit in before making my way back to Mexico in October. The day of my departure, April 11, I happened to fall into conversation in the street with a woman from Zipolite who lived in Tapachula, where her husband was stationed as a soldier. Back in town for the Easter holidays, this woman reported with swooping hand gestures that migrants had been wreaking unprecedented havoc as of late, burning Inami offices and even Siglo XXI to the ground. Precisely none of this was true, of course—but it was certainly more interesting to seekers of sensational news than that migrants in the infamous *ciudad-cárcel*/jail city had been agitating for basic rights.

The woman predicted that Tapachula was now in for a lot more drama, what with Salvadoran President Nayib Bukele's renewed declaration of the "war on gangs," which, she said, would surely send all the gang members running north for the Mexican border. Just two weeks earlier, Bukele had imposed a state of emergency following a tremendous spike in homicides unseen since the civil war era—a result, it turned out, of a collapse in negotiations between the gangs and Bukele's very own administration. Her prediction of impending chaos not-withstanding, the woman pronounced Bukele a world hero and the architect of a no-nonsense carceral policy that all regional leaders should emulate.

Indeed, if Tapachula was "jail city," El Salvador was incarceration nation—and, seven weeks into the state of emergency in May, the head of the Salvadoran National Civil Police took to Twitter to broadcast that "more than 31,000 terrorists" had thus far been apprehended. As in any good "war on terror," there had been plenty of collateral damage—like twenty-one-year-old musician Elvin Josué Sánchez Rivera, who was interned at the beginning of April at Izalco prison northwest of San

Salvador and who died a few weeks later. His family's request for an autopsy was refused, but Sánchez Rivera's body was covered in bruises.

Under the state of emergency, the Bukele regime hurriedly enacted a "special law" allowing for the rampant construction of new jails. Another wildly ambiguous law criminalizing the sharing of information about gangs also sped through the Salvadoran parliament. With truthful journalism thus conveniently outlawed along with any substantive discussion of Salvadoran reality, I opted to tell the airport immigration official in San Salvador that I had come to the country to take surfing lessons.

And yet even surfing can sometimes be terrorism, as I learned from a Salvadoran surfer and psychologist in his mid-thirties—we'll call him Julio—who had himself been swept up in the mass detention frenzy and had spent six days at the sweetly dubbed "El Penalito," or little prison, in the Salvadoran capital. As the *New York Times* noted, El Penalito had become "ground zero for perhaps the most aggressive police crackdown in the Central American country's history."

When I met Julio one afternoon in San Salvador for oversized beers, he told me that his cell at El Penalito had initially contained some fifty-five other people, from tattooed gang members to an eighty-four-year-old deaf man to a sixteen-year-old boy. A number of street vendors had also apparently been scooped up from the city center and hastily branded as gang associates, which was not only an efficient way for police to fulfill detention quotas mandated by the state of emergency but also to socially cleanse the downtown area to appeal to the international Bitcoin investor crowd—inside whose asses Bukele's tongue was permanently lodged.

Inside the cell, it was at first so crowded that it was impossible to sit or lie down. The toilet consisted of a hole in the ground. On account of his light skin and obvious relative socioeconomic advantage, Julio said, a few of the inmates suspected that the police had planted him there as an informant, but the gang member in charge in the cell looked out for him, just as he looked out for the eighty-four-year-old and the sixteen-year-old. This same gang member also ensured that everyone got their fair share of food at mealtimes and, after some of the prisoners had been transferred out of the cell, drew up a sleeping arrangement whereby everyone had someone else's feet in their face but which was at least preferable to standing up twenty-four hours a day.

Julio's cellmates nicknamed him "Tarzan," then promoted him to "Aquaman" and finally "El Profe"—"The

Teacher"—when he began offering instructions on physical exercises that could be performed in cramped spaces. Many of his cellmates had never even seen the sea, and were intrigued by his tales of surfing. Many of his cellmates had seen family members killed or raped.

According to Julio, had he not been so "white," he would not have been released from El Penalito in six days. In fact, he said, his family would probably never have heard from him again. Though he was still visibly shaken from his experience—worrying about the possibility of being out after dark and detained at police checkpoints on the road—his stint behind bars had served an educational purpose, providing psychological insights into a deranged regime's war on poverty. He had, he said, grasped more fully that gangs are an effect rather than the cause of a fundamentally violent system—one that is masterfully curated by the U.S., which in addition to backing right-wing atrocities worldwide has also set the standard for manically incarcerating poor people.

And while it should not take a psychologist to recognize that gang members are people, too, it is now effectively illegal in El Salvador to acknowledge their humanity—or to so much as acknowledge that there is a straightforward politico-socioeconomic explanation for their existence. The government's relentless portrayal of its prison population as savage terrorist-animals—including elderly deaf men and teenage boys—makes it even easier to deny them human rights.

It's anyone's guess as to whether we'll actually make it to the twenty-second century. But as things currently stand in the twenty-first, it seems there is sometimes more humanity behind bars than beyond them.

ABOUT THE AUTHOR

Belén Fernández is a columnist for *Al Jazeera* and a contributing editor at *Jacobin*, and has written for *The New York Times, Current Affairs, Middle East Eye*, and other venues. She is the author of *Checkpoint Zipolite: Quarantine in a Small Place, Exile: Rejecting America and Finding the World*, and *The Imperial Messenger: Thomas Friedman at Work*.